Southern Vampires

13 DEEP-FRIED BLOODCURDLING TALES

BY KARYN KAY ZWEIFEL

SWEETWATER
PRESS

SWEETWATER
PRESS

This edition published for Sweetwater Press by arrangement with
Crane Hill Publishers and Cliff Road Books.

ISBN-13: 978-1-58173-669-4
ISBN-10: 1-58173-669-X

Printed in U.S.A.

TABLE OF CONTENTS

For everyone who believed in me:
Doug, Kathryn, Jan, Jack, Kay, Brett, David, and Ellen

OLD SUE AND HER FRIENDS

he South has a long and honorable tradition of hauntings, mysterious apparitions, and unexplained phenomena. But when I was approached to collect the stories for this book, my first thought was "Southern *vampires*? No way!" Indeed, some well-known authorities on vampires told me early in my research that no Southern vampires existed. One day though, I discovered a mention of Old Sue, the slave vampire from a plantation somewhere in the Deep South. From then on, stories poured in from all sides.

I have collected these stories purely for their entertainment value. I did not intend in any way to portray a particular lifestyle as glamorous or desirable. The twentieth-century vampires I encountered seemed, if anything, to be slightly less happy than their non-blood-drinking peers.

Twelve of the stories included here are based on fact. I remained true to what details I knew in the more historical stories, but I "filled in" some that were beyond collecting. In a few stories, I altered some of the details to avoid causing unnecessary pain or publicity to the family and friends of those involved. And sometimes I took the bare skeleton of a story and fleshed it out the way I imagined it might have happened.

Drinking blood is not as bizarre an activity as it might seem at first. True gourmets won't order their steaks any way but rare. Ancient warriors believed eating the heart of a worthy opponent would grant them the strength of their vanquished foe. Blood pudding, or blood sausage, is a common, if unappetizingly named, dish. And Holy Communion, the most sacred ritual of all in the Christian church, centers around symbols of blood and flesh. Blood is, after all, the very essence of life.

How one obtains that blood is another matter entirely. And not every vampire requires an infusion of the red stuff to remain vital. Psychic vampires simply suck out the essence of their victim's spirit, gaining much pleasure in the process. I imagine there are more of these vampires around than is commonly acknowledged.

I hope you will find these stories truly entertaining. I also hope they will spark the realization that holding a narrow view of the world, a restricted sense of possibilities, means missing many things that are quite delightful. Denying the existence of the Devil, fairies, angels, Santa Claus, vampires, or any fantastic creature is to bind yourself to a world devoid of magic, a world that has lost the ability to hold grand schemes of good and evil and so challenge each of us to reach beyond our limitations.

There are many people who helped make this book a reality. The staff at the Birmingham Public Library was always ready to answer my questions. The librarians in the Social Sciences Department were particularly kind, and the staff of the Tutwiler Collection/Southern History was always patient with my sometimes odd requests for information.

The staff at the West Avenue Branch of the Newport News Public Library was very helpful, and Connie and Trinnette at the University of New Orleans Library were considerate enough to help on a holiday weekend. Everywhere I traveled, people were interested and eager to help, and I appreciate their assistance.

Eric Held and the Vampire Information Exchange Network gave me many clues, and Norrine Dresser, author of *American Vampires*, unearthed the story about Old Sue, which got me started on the whole project. Dr. Harriet Amos Doss, Associate Professor of History at the University of Alabama at Birmingham, gave me invaluable assistance with historic details from the mid-nineteenth century. Any errors or omissions are my own.

My family and friends were enthusiastic and supportive, and without their love and understanding, this book would never have been completed.

Southern Vampires

The Slumber Party

ommy, get in here!" The
television set was blaring, its black-and-white screen more fuzz than picture. "This is something you'll tell your children about!" In the cozy living room, a soft woman in her early thirties, her hair painstakingly crafted into a high, cylindrical shape, sat with her arm around an older man.

The kitchen was long and narrow with a table at one end and a door leading to the garage at the other. It was full of shadows. On the table, just out of sight of the living room and its occupants, sat a package of hamburger meat, nearly thawed, for tomorrow night's dinner.

"What are you doing, Tommy?" his mother screeched again. On the television set, the announcer's voice was reaching a fevered pitch of excitement.

Tommy was small for a seven-year-old. In the darkness indirectly lit by the TV set in the living room, his angular hand snaked across the table. Almost of their own volition, his slender fingers slipped under the cellophane wrap and embedded themselves in the cold, bloody meat. Quickly, ears alert to any sound of movement from the living room, he stuffed the dripping particles into his mouth, trying not to slurp too loudly. Again he reached into the package, eagerly this time, without hesitation. The sensation of blood upon his tongue gave him a delicious, savage thrill, a feeling that reverberated throughout his entire body.

"Tommy?" The overhead light snapped on and the boy jerked back, frightened. His hand still dripped blood. Red tendrils of meat and juices trailed out of his mouth onto the table.

1

"Oh God!" His stepfather recoiled in disgust. "Clean yourself up! Here!" He thrust a towel at the boy and then laughed nervously at his reaction. "I like my burgers rare too, boy, but not *that* rare!"

Tommy hastily ran the towel over his face and permitted his stepfather to lead him to the living room.

"Tranquility Base to Mission Control," the tinny voice from the television said, just as the two entered the living room. "The Eagle has landed."

"You're just in time," breathed Tommy's mother. "It's happening now!"

The picture on the small screen was so cluttered with snow and other interference that Tommy had to squint to see the ridiculously small craft settle on the surface of the moon. All he could think about was that feeling ... and how he could make it come again.

For most of the time over the next seven years, Tommy was an ordinary boy in his hometown of Ransom, Tennessee. He was perhaps a little quieter than most and spent a lot of time alone, but people attributed his solitary behavior to the sad loss of his father at such an early age.

"It's a good thing his mother remarried," they'd say. "And isn't his baby sister a little angel!"

Soon after the moon landing that July night, his mother had brought home a blanket-wrapped bundle. "It's your baby sister, Tommy," she squealed. "Aren't you *happy?*" That bundle soon consumed all her time and her husband's time too, but that didn't bother Tommy too much. His stepfather had become a little awkward around Tommy since the meat incident. He was too hearty, too likely to slap Tommy on the back and laugh, to make the boy comfortable. And yet at odd moments, Tommy would catch his stepfather staring at him with a curious gleam in his eyes, as if he were trying to see through the boy's skin to his soul within.

So Tommy would retreat to his little room, where he kept a box of Crayola crayons—the deluxe, 64-color box, with a built-in sharpener—and stacks of cheap, off-white newsprint sheets the size of typing paper. He would draw whatever was in his mind, usually dragons and knights, often with terrible wounds, the flesh laid open to the bone. Or

2

sometimes he would draw battle scenes with piles of dead on either side, limbs blasted off and heads severed, gore dripping off the page. As he got older, he began to draw women, faint and wounded, their lips slightly parted.

The various shades of red in his crayon box were all half the size of the other crayons, and he liked to experiment with his mother's viciously red nail enamel, which tore the flimsy paper. He loved her red lipsticks, which gave a realistic texture, but were too often discovered missing.

One afternoon when he was running home from school, his finger caught on a nail in a fence post and tore. His instinctive reaction was to put his finger in his mouth to stop the bleeding. At once, the taste of his own blood spurting onto his tongue made him dizzy with an unexpected pleasure. He abruptly sat down on the sidewalk and sucked his finger until it no longer yielded the sweet essence.

After that, Tommy would find a way to slightly cut himself once or twice a month, in the privacy of his bedroom or the bathroom. The intensity of his pleasure was heightened by the secrecy and dread that accompanied it. He knew that if he were ever caught, his sunny, uncritical mother would be shocked. And such a discovery would only confirm the dark suspicions he sometimes glimpsed in his stepfather's eyes.

Tommy satisfied his cravings in other ways, too. He would sometimes sneak to the refrigerator late at night and pilfer a piece or two of raw meat. And he became adept at sliding steaks and chopped beef into his trousers at the grocery store and then sauntering out after purchasing a loaf of bread or a bottle of milk for his mother.

He rarely played with his baby sister, but whenever he heard her wail in distress, he would run to her side. If she'd fallen and scraped a knee or elbow, he would quickly lap off the blood, the light pressure of his tongue tickling her and making her laugh and forget the pain of her injury.

"You're so good with little Susie, Tommy!" his mother would exclaim. "You're my little helper!"

When Tommy was fifteen, Susie had her first slumber party. She was eight, and so were two of her friends. The third one was nine, with tiny budding breasts and long, shapely legs. Tommy stayed in his bedroom most of the evening, while the girls squealed and giggled and played Peter Frampton records in the living room.

Tommy was restless. He had cut himself the night before, but it hadn't brought him the same depth of satisfaction it usually did. He paced his bedroom, sometimes pausing to stare out the window at the tar-black night beyond.

The reflection of his teeth gleamed white back at him, and he bared them, imagining the taste of raw bloody flesh. Perhaps a raw steak or some hamburger meat might soothe the craving that was racking his thin frame. As soon as the girls went to sleep, he'd make his way to the kitchen and see what he could find.

"All right, girls, lights out!" shouted Tommy's stepfather with an air of joviality. "This is a slumber party, not a stay-awake party. Let's all get some shut-eye."

Tommy winced at his stepfather's heavy-handed attempt at humor. Now there, he thought, was a useless piece of meat.

Tommy turned out his own light and cracked open his bedroom door. He sat in the dark, waiting impatiently for the girls to stop talking. Their sleeping bags were arrayed in a semicircle around the fireplace, so Tommy would have to step over one or two of them on his way to the kitchen.

The girls whispered and laughed so long that his stepfather entered the living room again. "Look," he said crossly, "I'm beginning to think I'll have to send you all home in order to get some sleep."

"Oh, no sir, Mr. Phillips," the girls chorused. "We'll be quiet, honest!"

Tommy hugged his midsection and bent over, suppressing a groan. Maybe he was coming down with something. He'd never felt so hollow, so achingly empty before. Just some red and dripping meat was all he needed.

At last, the girls' giggles faded into the rhythmic breathing of sleep. In a half-crouch, Tommy began to make his way to the kitchen. The oldest girl's sleeping bag was spread out, blocking his access to the kitchen door. Just as he was about to step over her, she stirred in her sleep.

4

Tommy froze, eyes glued to her face to see if she would awaken. As he stared, he noticed the graceful line of her jaw, leading so smoothly to the silken skin of her neck. There, above the sweet bulge of the collarbone, beat her jugular vein. Tommy's eyes fixed there. Mesmerized, he felt his mouth go dry as he pictured the flow of life's essence pumping ceaselessly just below the surface of the skin. His need grew so fiercely he rocked back on his heels, as if struck by a blow from an unseen hand.

His breath labored, he stood and backed away. Crossing that boundary would change his life. He quickly stepped over the girl's prostrate body and into the kitchen beyond. In the refrigerator he found a roast, defrosting for tomorrow's Sunday dinner. With shaking hands, he took a knife and severed one-third of it, careless in his desperate need. He crammed the bloody meat into his mouth, tearing it viciously, hungrily. When it was gone, he stood in front of the Frigidaire, panting slightly. He still felt empty, but knew what he needed. He only had to overcome his fear in order to satisfy his hunger.

Taking the knife, he crept softly to where the girl lay sprawled in her sleeping bag. Holding his breath, he knelt over her, pausing a second to make certain she still slept. While his heart roared, he ever so carefully slipped the knife rapidly over the vein, barely nicking the skin. A drop, then two, then a thin stream of thick blood flowed out, burgundy in the dim light. He bent over her, lightly lapping at her neck, while she moaned softly in her sleep.

Again he rocked back on his heels, this time with his eyes glowing, filled with a pleasure so intense he could barely control his moans of ecstasy. The blood quickly stopped flowing—it was only a superficial cut—and Tommy realized with mounting excitement that he had begun a whole new life, defined by terror and blood.

He knew, of course, he couldn't find sleeping, defenseless girls just anywhere. And to seek his pleasure with anyone other than people who were unaware of his ministrations would be to invite disaster. So over the next three years, Tommy only enjoyed the overwhelmingly satisfying sensation four or five times.

Once, at summer camp, he stole quietly into the girls' cabin, where ten or twelve were sleeping peacefully. The smell of so much young flesh nearly overcame his senses, but he managed to slink silently to the bedside of one young girl. He had his knife out, ready to make the cut, when the girl in the next bed sneezed violently.

He immediately dropped to his knees, ready to roll under the bed and hide. He was undiscovered, but his hands were shaking so violently he didn't dare try to cut his intended victim. This was the closest he came to detection in the three years before he left his home in that small Tennessee town.

He came to be known as "Tom" rather than "Tommy," but he still kept to himself wherever he lived. He began to date, and was fortunate in the type of women who were drawn to his slender good looks.

Amanda was typical. She liked to twist her long, silky hair into a knot, exposing her slender throat to Tom's covetous eyes. On their second date, Tom took her up to a ridge that overlooked the lights of the Southern city he now called home. They talked aimlessly, but the air between them was charged with an intoxicating tension.

At last, Tom pulled her close to him and began to kiss her, softly at first, then more demanding. Mick Jagger was moaning in the background as Tom's lips moved slowly, sensuously around the curve of Amanda's jaw and down her throat. She responded, her strong fingers cradling his head. "Pleased ta meetcha," mocked the singer on the radio. "Hope ya guessed my name. . ."

Tom could no longer contain his hunger. He plunged his sharp incisors into the supple skin of her neck, then lapped gently at the wound just as he had his baby sister's wounds, so long ago. Amanda yelped in surprise but made no protest, and they continued their embrace after Tom had luxuriated in the dark thrill of her blood.

Their relationship continued for some months. Sometimes Amanda would murmur into his ear that she liked him to nibble on her neck, but he did not always indulge himself. They parted company eventually, but Tom soon found other women willing to play an unwitting role in his secret life.

In 1981 he began to hear rumors of a strange disease, apparently communicated by blood and other bodily fluids. When the full extent of the horrors of AIDS became known, Tom decided to give up his strange passion, no matter what the cost. He decided it couldn't be worth his life.

The first few months of abstinence were only just bearable. Tom threw himself into his work and began to jog and lift weights at a nearby gym. He refused the advances of all women, not trusting himself to leave their necks untouched. One evening, though, in late fall, the moon hung low and full in the sky, framed by the stark black branches of trees stripped bare. Suddenly the hunger tore into him like a knife, making him cry out with pain as he ran around the perimeter of the park near his apartment.

The pain's intensity grew, and Tom was forced to stop running. He crouched over holding his midsection, groaning. The brunt of the attack passed after what seemed an eternity, and he limped slowly back to his apartment. There, he grabbed his billfold and ventured out into the night.

The butcher at a local specialty shop was just leaving for the night, but Tom, with a forced grin on his drawn face, convinced him to special-cut four steaks from a side of beef just delivered that day. He watched through the glass partition, leaning on the display case, his lips parted and his breath coming harder than it should. He thanked the man and then nearly ran to the register to pay for his bounty.

In his car, he hunched over the steering wheel, tearing at the meat and feeling the juices run down either side of his mouth. He sensed someone staring, and he looked up to see the butcher peering curiously through the windshield on his way to his own car. Tom snarled, and the man backed away, hands held in the air, as if to reassure Tom that he meant no harm.

The meat barely assuaged Tom's terrible hunger. Since then, he has rarely gone without blood for more than three months at a time. Any longer, and his hunger becomes uncontrollable. Sometimes he can find a woman who is "safe"; other times, he finds the freshest possible meat. He never returned to that particular store, and he feels an overwhelming need to keep his appetites and his pleasures a secret from everyone around him.

Tom is not the only one out there. Daylight doesn't bother him, he can see his reflection in the mirror, and he doesn't sleep in a coffin. So if you should meet a charming man who is a little shy and has a particular fondness for nibbling at your neck, don't be too surprised. He might be looking for someone a lot like you.

OLD SUE

eads of sweat glistened on arms, legs, torsos, faces; each drop caught and held a miniature reflection of the firelight before flying off into the darkness, like cold sparks. The people flung themselves around and around in reckless abandon, fueled by the driving rhythms of a traveling fiddler. Beyond the circle of light thrown by the wild bonfire, the cotton fields stood vigil in stony silence.

Two broomsticks lay side by side, shoved nearly out of sight in the dirt near a cabin doorstep. Half an hour earlier, they had been the center of attention as Sara and Edward faced each other. The preacher had traveled all the way from Memphis.

"Dark and stormy may come de wedder;

I jines dis he-male an' dis she-male togedder.

Let none, but Him dat makes de thunder,

Put dis he-male and she-male asunder.

I dare for 'nounce you bofe de same.

Be good, go 'long, an' keep up yo' name.

De broomstick's jumped, de world not wide.

She's now yo' own. Salute yo' bride!"

Edward jumped over the broomstick handle held about a foot off the ground, and Sara jumped at the same time, landing next to him in a swirl of skirts as they clasped their hands.

"Praise de Lawd!" shouted someone in the watching crowd, and everyone began heaping blessings and advice on the couple. Children darted in and out of the crowd, shrieking and carrying on their own private ceremony as significant to them as the schemes and plans of the adults who ignored them.

"Where be Old Sue?" Sara asked, laughing as she disentangled herself from the crowd. "She say she gib me de secret to long life on my weddin' day. You see her tonight, Sam?"

"Naw," answered a tall, perilously thin man with skin so dark it seemed to soak up the light, instead of reflecting it. "I reckon she don' wanna see no preacher-man."

"You don' believe them stories 'bout her, do you? She just an ol' woman."

"No one lib dat long widdout some help." Sam replied, evasively. "But I ain't gonna jinx yur wedding day wif dis talk. Get 'long, and don' worry 'bout ol' Sue. I wouldn't want her secrets, I were you."

Sara shook her head, smiling, as she turned back to the crowd of folks celebrating her wedding night. Tomorrow would be just another day, but tonight was hers, and she would clutch these memories tight with a surprising fierceness. Nothing could spoil the event, not Sam's strange comments or Evie's drunken screeches.

"How'd Evie git her hainds on that likker, anyways?" Sara linked her arm through Edward's, on the edge of a group clustered around the woman who would alternately sob and scream obscenities.

Edward shrugged. "Dunno. When you works in the House, you kin git yur hainds on mos' anythang, I reckon. When they find that whiskey gone, somebody'll get a whippin', fer shore."

Just then, Evie pushed her way to the couple and thrust her face into Sara's.

"You thinks you happy," she hissed. "You gots what you want. A husband, mebbe a baby. But you looks at me good, girl—you see what a stumblin' piece o' misery I is—you be here soon. I promise you." The combined stench of whiskey and rage made Sara's head swim. As she staggered backward Edward caught her arm.

"Now Evie, you calm down. Thass no way to treat a bride on her weddin' night!" John, Evie's husband, grabbed Evie and pushed her out of the crowd, down the row of houses, and into a cabin closest to the fields. The other slaves could hear Evie's whimpering start, even before John slammed the flimsy door.

About forty revelers were left in the wide dirt clearing between the cabin rows, and Edward nodded his head curtly to the fiddler, who struck up another tune. As she danced, Sara deliberately put out of her mind the malice in Evie's voice. After the fiddler had finished, Sara went to the water barrel for a drink. She jumped when a hand touched her elbow.

"Didn't mean ter scare ya," Dicy said. "Gimme dat dipper. Dancin's thirsty work.

"Don't let dat ol' wicked Evie bother you," Dicy continued. She had an uncanny way of picking up on Sara's thoughts sometimes. "You know since her baby gone, she not quite right in the haid."

"I think she waren't right in the haid before dat," Sara replied. "I think she did away wid dat baby. She crazy."

"If she kilt it, she hid it good. Nobody's found it yet, and John near tore up the place lookin'. Let's git sumpin' to eat. You try the chicken yet? I fried it special fer you." Taking the younger woman by the arm, Dicy led her to a long table littered with the remains of a grand wedding feast.

The children ran back into the clearing, shrieking again, and Dicy looked up sharply. There was a razor-edged note of panic to their screams that hadn't been present before. She had three children, and the youngest one ran to her, sobbing.

"Shush, now, shush. What you get into, lil' bit?" Dicy dropped to her knees and smoothed back the four-year-old's hair. "Shush, now. I cain't unnerstan' what you sayin', you cryin' too hard."

The other children gathered around Dicy's familiar figure. "It nearly got us," shouted one little boy. "I ain't never seen nothin' so big! We's jist havin' a little fun, and then dis thing comes down, I think it bit 'im!"

Dicy's hands moved a little more frantically now, running over the scalp, face, shoulders of her youngest son. "You hurt, boy? Point it out to me. Show me," she commanded. The boy's wild sobs slowed, and nearly stopped, until his mother's questing fingers found a puncture just below his earlobe. She swung him up onto her hip and strode over to the fire,

11

for a closer examination of the wound, as his sobs climbed the scales of intensity.

Assured that the blood was no longer flowing freely, she turned angrily to the oldest boy in the crowd, one arm still wrapped around her baby.

"You bin throwin' rocks, Percy?" she demanded. "Dis look like he got hit by a rock. You coulda put his eye out, and what happen to a blind slave, huh boy?" In her fury, she approached the boy, who stammered but held his ground.

"No'm," he whispered. "I sware. We ain't bin throwin' no rocks. Sumpin' bit 'im. It fell outta de sky and like to have carried 'im off."

"He's right, Mama." A skinny girl with pigtails moved toward Dicy. "We was playin' and den there was a big shadow, like a cloud over de moon. I heered 'im scream and heered wings, like a big hoot owl."

Some of the adults in the crowd muttered and made the sign against the evil eye. The hoot owl was often a portent of death—and certainly never brought good fortune.

The little boy had recovered enough to nestle closer to his mama and put his arms around her neck tightly. "Mebbe it was a bat, Mama," he said. "I tol' 'em not to go throwin' rocks at dem bats we saw."

Dicy whirled around to face the children with new accusations, but they had melted into the shadows of the quarters, slipping off to the protection of their own mamas. Dicy was left with her band of three standing around her skirts, and she had to be content with mumbled threats about taking care of their baby brother next time.

Sara and Edward's wedding was the last big celebration in the quarters for a while. Cotton prices were sinking fast, and every slave heard rumors of others being sold and sent away to an unknown future. These whispered stories set everyone's nerves on edge.

Sara's belly waxed full and round; the moon had temporarily ceased its hold over her body, superseded by a stronger force. As she nurtured the slave quarter's youngest life within her, she turned to the quarter's oldest life more and more frequently.

"How old is you, anyway?" she asked curiously. She squatted next to Sue's rocker placed on the doorstep of the woman's one room cabin, its location in the center of the quarters a subtle sign of the old woman's status. Sara's cabin was three doors down, closest to the stables and the big house beyond.

"Laws, I don' know, chile," laughed the withered old woman. "I reckon I be a hunnert, a hunnert 'n' two. My mama used to tell me 'bout Africa. She follered the ol' religion there."

"They say the master never beat you," Sara said, idly tracing patterns in the dirt. "He afraid of your mama?"

Above her, unseen, the old crone's features twitched, twisted into a grimace of pain or maybe anger.

"Sara!" Edward's voice boomed down the narrow dirt street of the quarters. "I'm hungry, woman!"

Sara scrambled awkwardly to her feet. "Oh, I's so tired I jest couldn't face cookin'," she gasped. "What'll I do, Mother Sue?"

Sue rocked placidly, hands laced over her thin frame. "I got some cold corn mush in there, chile," she said. "That'll do. And come by termorrow when you get back from the fields. I got a tonic fer you. Your time be here soon."

Edward muttered at the sight of another cold supper. "You spen' too much time wid dat ol' witch," he said.

"She ain't no witch, Edward!" Sara snapped. "She mo' help to me than anybody!"

"Dicy used to be your friend," Edward persisted.

"Well she and you both ain't got nuthin' good to say about Mother Sue. I be tired of your superstitions an' tale-tellin'." Sara flung herself down on the pallet in the corner, turning her face to the wall and lacing her fingers over her belly, which quivered and moved with increasing frequency as the days went by.

Next evening, Dicy gave her youngest son an iron kettle of beans seasoned with fatback. "Take this up to Sara's cabin," she commanded. "Mind you don't dawdle, now!" Her smile weakened the sternness of her words as she watched his small figure receding, lugging the heavy kettle with both hands, inches above the ground. The sun had just dipped below the horizon; bats fluttered and swooped as shadows transformed the familiar lines and shapes of the quarters into something insubstantial.

Dicy turned to get back to her evening's work inside the cabin. Just then, a shrill cry pierced the evening, sending a dagger of fear slicing into her heart.

"Willie!" she shouted, running toward the stables, in the direction of Sara's cabin. "Where you be, boy?" Fright added a sharp note to her voice. Just then, his slight figure burst out of the shadows.

She scooped him up, trying to still the frantic movement of his limbs as he struggled to free himself from her grasp. His face was contorted into a rictus of fear. He seemed not to know his mother or his home as she carried him inside.

"He havin' a fit," Dicy said grimly to her other two children, who stood gaping at their younger brother.

"What happened, Mama?" whispered Eliza, Dicy's daughter.

"I dunno." Dicy pointed to a patchwork quilt on a pallet next to the wall. "Gimme dat." She bundled Willie tightly in the quilt, her rocking and soothing noises seeming to have little effect on the boy. But slowly, the boy's frantic struggle subsided into trembling, and then he fell into a light and troubled sleep. Dicy stood vigil over her son as he moaned and thrashed his way through the hours of darkness.

"She flies," he moaned. "Oh, her wings, dey hurt," he whimpered. He woke up, and recognition dawned in his eyes as he looked up at Dicy. He clung to her. "Don't let her get me, Mama," he pleaded.

"Who, Willie, who?" Dicy whispered.

"It's Old Sue, Mama," he replied. "She flies, she wants to hurt me, ooh, mama, don't . . . " His voice trailed off as his eyes rolled back in his head. Dicy shook him roughly.

"Don't, boy," she commanded. "Come back, Willie!" After what felt like an eternity, his eyes opened again, his breath rasping in his throat.

"I lost that kettle, Mama," he whispered. "I sorry."

"Yes, yes," she crooned, rocking him and stroking his head. "Yes, yes, lil' bit," she crooned as the first pale tendrils of dawn trickled over the windowsill.

Dicy's eyes were just closing when Edward crossed her threshold.

"It's her time, Dicy," he blurted. "Sara, she need you!"

Dicy eyed him sourly. "She ask for me, Edward?"

"Well, not exactly," he stammered. "But she would, I think."

"She be pretty mad at me last week," Dicy said, gently laying Willie down and rising to gather her things. "She say I be bad-mouthin' ol' Sue."

Edward looked at an iron kettle dangling from his hands, as if he didn't know how it came to be there. "This your kettle?" he asked. "Ol' Sue say she found it outside her door this morning."

Dicy snatched the kettle and flung it toward the hearth. "Let's go," she said dourly. "Eliza, you get breakfas' fo your brother now." She bundled Willie, still sleeping, into a quilt and thrust him into Edward's arms.

All morning, Sara paced the narrow confines of her windowless cabin, wincing slightly at each new assault of pain. Willie played, listlessly, in a corner. Dicy had gone off to the fields to work.

"It'll be a while, yet," she assured Sara. "When it git so bad you cain't help but scream, send Willie to get me, hear?"

A few hours after the sun had slipped past its peak, Sara's face turned ashen gray as she struggled to contain her cries of pain.

"Go git yer mama, Willie," she gasped to the boy. He didn't speak but scampered out the door and between the cabins, heading straight for the fields. Before he reached the last shack, Sara's wracking screams tore through the silence that lay over the nearly empty quarters. A dark form, bent and thin, slipped with an eerie agility into Sara's doorway.

Dicy and Willie made their way back from the fields. As they got closer to the quarters, Dicy gently scolded her son. "I don' hear no screamin' boy," she chided. "She'd better be ready fo' me or. . ."

Just then Willie inhaled with a little shriek and shrank back into Dicy's skirts. She looked up, sharply, just in time to see a shadowy form flit between two cabins.

"What's wrong, boy?" she asked. "Talk to me." He'd talk sooner or later she decided as she turned into Sara's door. Sara lay still, and Dicy's eyes blinked, adjusting to the dim light inside.

"Look, Dicy," Sara whispered. "I got me a baby boy." She held up a tightly swaddled infant.

"How?" Dicy stammered. "Who birthed him?"

"Mother Sue did." Sara's eyes glittered in the darkness. "She heard me and came to help."

Willie whimpered and scrambled up onto Dicy's hip. "Well, I'm glad she help you, Sara," Dicy said in a strangled voice. "I'll just, I'll just start some supper for you 'n' Edward then."

Just at dusk, a few hours after Dicy had returned to her cabin, Sara's screams shattered the peace of early evening. Dicy picked up her skirts and ran helter-skelter to Sara's cabin, Willie still clinging mutely to her hip.

Sara was huddled in the corner, shuddering, clutching the baby as she sobbed. Edward crouched next to her, begging her to speak.

"What happened?" Dicy asked.

"I dunno," Edward shrugged helplessly. "I went to git some water an' when I got back she waz cryin'."

"Gimme that baby, girl," Dicy coaxed. "It's okay. We take care of you."

"She flies, Dicy," Sara whimpered. "She want my baby."

Willie, clinging now to Dicy's back as she bent over the other woman, stiffened.

"You tired, honey," Dicy said. "Havin' dat baby wear you out. You seein' things."

Sara's eyes lost their cloudy look of fear and became fierce and hot. "No, Dicy. She want my baby. But she cain't have him." She clutched the baby so tightly it began to wail in protest.

"At least git yourself over here on your blanket. The baby be more comfortable here."

Sara allowed herself to be led to the pallet on the dirt floor but wouldn't lie down. The baby nursed, quiet again, as Sara watched Dicy and Edward busy themselves about the cabin, stirring up the fire, setting the two rough stools upright again, and dishing out two plates of corn mush.

Sara didn't sleep that night but sat upright and watched the door. At dawn, she was knocking at Dicy's door. "Dicy, I need some red peppers," she said.

"Don' worry about your supper, girl," Dicy protested. "You an' Edward can eat with us. You git your strength back first."

"I ain't cookin' with 'em, Dicy," Sara said quietly.

Realization crossed slowly across Dicy's face. "You think. . ." She pulled Sara into the cabin and shut the door. "You think ol' Sue. . ." She quickly made the sign against evil.

"I saw her, Dicy," Sara said. "She flew, and I saw her eyes. I know it was her, and she was comin' for my baby. Edward heard someone say she can turn herself into a cat, an' nobody knows how old she really is, an' I think she been plannin' to git my baby since before I was married."

"Sssshh, now," Dicy gathered up the younger woman into her arms. "It'll be all right, now."

"Them peppers all I know to keep my baby safe," Sara whimpered. "They say to put 'em in his socks and no witch or vampire will git 'im, an' I'm afraid I cain't stay awake to watch over 'im every night, an' I don't know what else to do."

"We git you them peppers right now, honey," Dicy said as she rummaged through her spices. "Here!" She triumphantly held up a short string of wizened red chile peppers. "Now, let's git on out to the fields before they come lookin' fer us!"

The next day, Sam stumbled over Sara's sleeping form, tucked away in a patch of weeds in the far corner of the cotton field.

"Mercy, chil'!" he exclaimed. "I didn't know if you was dead or alive!"

Sara moaned and stirred, causing the baby strapped across her chest to whimper in reply.

"Why you out here sleepin', girl?" Sam asked. "They catch you, they sell you for bein' lazy, you know."

"I cain't sleep at night, Sam," Sara cried. "Ol' Sue gonna come git my baby, an' I gotta watch out fer her!"

Sam knelt next to the young woman. "I would worry about what comes to get you in the daylight, girl. That'll kill you quicker." He straightened up as he heard a shouted command behind him. "The Lord watch over you, honey." He turned and left her curled in a nest of weeds.

No one caught Sara sleeping that day, and she returned to the cabin with Edward an hour before dusk.

"What we gonna eat tonight, Sara?" Edward asked, afraid he already knew the answer.

"I don' care, Edward," Sara replied wearily. "I think there's some left-over mush or sumpin' in the kettle. I just want to ketch some sleep before it gits dark."

True to her word, she curled up on the pallet as soon as they returned, and soon slept soundly. So soundly that she didn't even hear the baby wake up and cry.

"Here, baby, now hush," Edward said, handling the baby awkwardly. "You a fine boy, like your daddy, heh?" he spoke softly as he marveled at the baby's tightly clenched, perfectly formed fists. "I bet you got fine little toes, too," he mused, and pulled off the knitted socks that Sara had made with care during her pregnancy.

Two red peppers fell to the ground, and Edward stooped to pick them up. "What's this?" he wondered. "You think I should spice up that old mush, boy?" He laughed softly. "Let's not wake your mama up. She so tired, she git mighty cranky."

Quietly, while playing with the baby, Edward ate his supper, spitting the husks of the peppers out onto the fire, where they hissed and spat back like a live creature. Then he lay the baby down next to Sara and lay close to them both, his big arm encircling his family as night fell down across the quarters.

Sara woke in the darkness with a start. "Where is he?" she shrieked, pummeling Edward's solidly sleeping form. "Where's my baby?"

Edward woke up, dazed. "What?"

Sara tore through the quarters that night, searching everywhere for her baby boy. Edward could barely restrain her from going up the hill to the big house during her search. All the while, she screamed and tore her hair, just like a crazy woman. She swore someone had taken that baby away, and she wouldn't rest until she found him. Exhausted, she slumped into sleep at dawn and didn't even hear Old Sue drag her rocking chair out to the stoop of the cabin next door.

"Morning, Sue," Sam nodded curtly as he passed her cabin. "You lookin' mighty spry this mornin'."

"Yes, my rheumatism done let up a little bit," she nodded, her fingers nimbly picking beans from the shell. "Why, today I feels like I could live another hunnerd years. Mercy, yes."

NEWPORT NEWS

vant to suck your bluuuud." The short, stocky man in his forties snickered as he nuzzled his head deep between the big blond's ear and her shoulder.

"Get off me, Billy," the woman complained good-naturedly, swatting at him. "You stink."

The man shrugged as he settled himself on a bar stool and wrapped a disproportionately large, scarred hand around a beer bottle.

"If you worked all day, you'd stink too, Candy."

"I do work. I'm just not an overpriced con artist like you."

"I earn every penny of it. If you tossed bricks around all day in 90 degree weather, you'd want sixteen dollars an hour, too."

"What's this vampire thing, Billy?" The bartender set another bottle of Bud down, watching as beads of sweat worked their way down to the polished surface of the bar.

"I'm a vampire," Billy said, watching their faces closely to gauge their reactions. "I just found out. See this?" He smoothed a newspaper clipping onto the bar's surface. It had been rolled in a cylinder and tucked in his shirt pocket, next to his cigarettes.

"I've got this rare disease, called 'por'. . . uh, 'porphyria.' You know how I've always said the light hurts my eyes? And how pale I always am, even though I work in the sun?"

"You just like the nightlife, Billy!" The woman guffawed and slapped him on the back, rocking him forward slightly.

"And I never could stand Italian food or any kind of garlic." Billy stabbed at the newspaper article with his forefinger to emphasize his point. "I've got this rare disease of the liver, and it means my blood needs a boost every now and then, see? So the doc gives me a shot of medicine, and it's made from. . ." he paused for effect, "human blood!"

The bartender shook his head and idly swiped his bar towel across the countertop. Candy shivered in mock terror. Billy looked pleased. He downed the rest of his beer, threw a five on the bar, and headed out the door.

"Keep the change, Will," he called over his shoulder as he left.

"That's why he keeps that job," Candy said. "He's too free with his money. He can't afford to do something that pays less." She patted her bright curls where Billy's head had briefly rested.

The bartender just smiled and pocketed his tip.

Outside, Charles William Brownell flinched as the last of the day's heat washed over him. Inside, in the air conditioning, it was easy to forget how miserable this Virginia summer was shaping up to be. He climbed into his battered green Chevy pickup and turned right, toward home.

Pulling into the 7-Eleven to pick up a six-pack, he saw a familiar car. A dusty brown Corolla, eleven years old but "with an engine good as new," he remembered with a smile. The owner came out of the store just as Billy got to the door.

"Hey, Jeff!"

"Billy! Hey, man, how's it goin'?" The skinny man, really just a boy, Billy thought, enthusiastically shook Billy's hand.

"How's the car running?"

"Just great. I can't tell you how big a difference that car's made to me."

Billy had paid seven hundred dollars for the car, after he and Jeff had gotten to know each other at a job site. The kid had been desperate for a car, and Billy had some money burning a hole in his pocket.

"Listen, I'm gonna get a six-pack. Why don't you follow me over to my place and we'll put a few back, maybe throw some burgers on the grill?"

Jeff grinned. "That'd be great." He fished his keys out of his pocket and turned to the Toyota. "You still live out by Deer Creek?"

Billy nodded.

"I'll just meet you there, then. Lemme stop by my house and tell them where I'm goin'."

"Still live with your folks?"

Jeff grimaced. "Yeah. The price is right though. It's free."

"See ya."

The sun was still bright but losing some of its fierceness when Billy arrived at his apartment. He cranked up the air conditioner and surveyed the living room. Crossed ceremonial swords, reproductions of Civil War relics, hung above the sagging brown sofa. A gray forage cap displaying the Confederate insignia decorated the top of the TV, which was by far the most expensive piece of furniture in the place. And, of course, a five-foot-wide Confederate flag draped the wall behind the dinette set. His mandolin sat in its case in the corner, and Billy thought he might play it tonight.

Jeff knocked on the door, and Billy handed him a beer. Later, when they went outside to grill hamburgers, they could hear the distant screams of children playing in the ball field at Deer Park. From this distance, their shrieks might have been calls of joy or terror. Billy felt replete with a calm sense of peace. He had his friends, his work, his own place, his music, and his Civil War collection.

The sun now hung low in a nest of full, fat clouds. Its sullen glow spilled over, painting the coastal flatlands in frivolous shades of purple, pink, and mauve. A few moments later, as the sun fell away, the color of the clouds darkened to an angry red. Their low-hanging pendulous forms seemed to be trailing crimson fingers from the dying sun.

"Some show, huh?" Billy turned to Jeff, but he was preoccupied with the leaping flames of the barbecue grill and the charred flesh that was soon to be their dinner.

Billy patted his shirt pocket, looking for a cigarette, and his fingers touched the cylinder of newsprint he'd tucked there earlier. Over their burgers, dripping hot grease on their fingers, he told Jeff what he'd learned about his strange disease.

Jeff stayed for a few hours more, and Billy picked his mandolin to the fast and furious bluegrass rhythms he loved. As he stood in the doorway, watching the boy's slender back as he walked to his car, he saw the moon had risen. The sweet white curve of the crescent moon overhead was a study in innocence, a startling contrast to the fury of the clouds in the earlier sunset hours.

As he drove home the next day, Billy caught flashes of silver over to his left. The broad James River and Chesapeake Bay enfolded Newport News like loving arms. Sometimes in the summer, the humidity and swarms of mosquitoes rising from the water made those arms feel suffocating, but Billy was glad to call the city home. Winters here were a lot more bearable than the snow and ice-encrusted horrors of a Massachusetts winter. A seagull cried overhead.

He jumped down from the cab in front of his apartment, cheerfully slamming his truck door and startling Mrs. Richey, his downstairs neighbor. She was dutifully pouring water on some leggy, wilting pansies.

"Mercy, look at you," she said, setting down the watering can.

Billy was dusted, head to foot, with clay-colored powder from the bricks he'd been handling since dawn. Trails of sweat snaked down his arms, face, and neck, leaving streaks of white skin exposed beneath the chalky red coating. It was a bizarre kind of photo-negative, a harbinger of carnage to come.

"You scared me half to death, Billy," she scolded. "And see if you can't keep those parties under control, will you?"

"What parties, Mrs. Richey?" Billy was genuinely puzzled.

"You know what I mean. Those boys, in and out at all hours, and that crazy music. I could call the police, you know." She puffed up, self righteously, and turned to go back inside her apartment.

"It's bluegrass, Mrs. Richey," he hollered at her retreating back. "It beats the hell out of Lawrence Welk!"

On Friday, payday, he stopped at the Anchor for a beer on his way home. Candy was there looking glum.

"What's up, Sweetlips?" he said, sliding onto the stool next to her.

"Well if it isn't my favorite vampire," crowed the bartender. He didn't even ask before he popped the top off a cold Bud and set it down in front of Billy.

"Don't call me that," Candy said to Billy. "I feel pretty sour right now."

"What's wrong?"

"Well that asshole I married is just about three months behind on the child support payments, and the bank called today to say they're gonna repossess my car. Whatever possessed me to marry that man, I don't have a clue." She drained the draft beer in front of her and started to stand up. Billy put a hand on her arm.

"How much?" he said.

Candy looked startled. "What?"

"How much does the bank want?"

"I owe for three payments, but it's a piece of shit anyway. I'll let them have it."

"You can't get to work without a car, Candy." Billy was reaching for his wallet. "Look, here's four hundred. That'll help, won't it?"

Candy shook her head and pushed his hand away. "I can't borrow money from you, Billy."

"Why not?" The bartender was watching with some amusement. "Everybody else does. We call him 'Bank Billy.'"

"I don't know when I can pay you back," she protested.

"Don't worry about it. When you catch up to your ex. Whenever."

"You're some kinda saint, Billy. I mean that." Candy was near tears.

"Aw, shucks." Billy scraped his feet on the carpet in mock humility. "Have another beer with me."

"I've got to pick up Carl Jr. at the baby-sitter's. I should rename him Billy Jr. You're worth a whole lot more than that jerk of a father he's got."

Billy watched Candy leave.

"Sad, isn't it?"

"Never marry, Billy," the bartender said solemnly. "You'll avoid all kinds of hell that way."

"No worry, Will. I won't. It's too late for me."

Jeff came over right after sunset, another bloody display of light and clouds. They threw a couple of steaks on the grill, and watched the sparks float up into the sky.

24

"Your new job going all right, Jeff?" Billy asked, craning his neck to look for the North Star.

"Ahh, I guess so. They treat me like some kind of slave, though. Do this, do that, fetch this, fetch that. I get sick of it. But the last time I quit, my mom about bitched me to death."

"Women are good at that."

"Yeah. I wish I didn't have to live with her."

"You said yourself, the rent's cheap enough."

"You got two bedrooms here, don'tcha?"

Billy was amused but tried not to let it show. "Nope. Just the one."

"Your rent's what, about three hundred?"

"Three-fifty, plus utilities. Why?"

"Well, I think I could afford half of that."

Billy sighed. "I like you, Jeff. But I like my privacy, too. Let's just leave things like they are, okay?"

"You don't understand what it's like." Jeff kicked at the ground. "She snoops through my stuff, and she's always bitching if I buy new clothes or something. She acts like she's so damn poor when I know she's not."

"Sometimes it's hard to be grown-up, Jeff." Billy didn't know if he was talking about the boy or the boy's mother. He suddenly felt old. Old enough, in fact, to be the boy's father.

"Let's eat."

After dinner, Jeff poked at the gory remains of his steak. "Do you ever wonder what it'd be like to really be a vampire?"

Billy stretched out on the sofa. "Nope."

Jeff came over to him, standing over the prone figure of his friend. "Have you ever tasted blood?"

"Nope." Billy eyed the boy curiously. "Have you?"

Jeff collapsed on the floor in nervous laughter. "Naaah."

On Saturdays, Mrs. Richey ventured out shortly after lunch, her collapsible shopping cart trailing obediently behind her like a gleaming, fleshless dog. Not two feet out of her door, she stopped short, staring in anger at the dull red twin tracks around her upstairs neighbor's door.

"Filthy habits," she said softly, shaking her head. Then, noticing his door was ajar, she pushed it open, calling up the stairway. "William Brownell, get your lazy self out here and clean up this mess!"

When her eyes adjusted to the dimness of the stairs, they widened in shock. In here, the tracks were a bright red. Nothing at all like brick dust. In fact, they glistened. Puddles, even pools of the substance dripped slowly down the stairs, saturating the light-gray carpet and slowly winding their way toward her feet.

Candy burst through the door of the Anchor, nearly pulling Carl Jr. off his feet as she whirled toward the bar.

"Candy, you know you can't bring him in here," Will protested mildly.

"Turn the TV on," she demanded. "I can't believe what I'm hearing."

"That's right!" screamed an announcer. "I said $7999 for a BRAND NEW Ford Escort!"

Will cocked an eyebrow at Candy. She drummed her fingers impatiently on the bar.

A chorus of women sang sweetly about the virtues of Pomoco Ford.

Will slid a cup full of maraschino cherries over to Carl Jr. just as the perky young woman from WAVY TV appeared on the screen.

"Our top story tonight is a gruesome mystery in Newport News. Police are looking for a Charles William Brownell and his green 1979 Chevrolet pickup truck. He is wanted for questioning in connection with a possible murder."

Candy was almost speechless with rage. "That's the most preposterous thing I've ever heard! Billy wouldn't hurt a fly!"

"What else did you hear, Candy? Was it on the radio?" Will had turned the sound down on the TV set as customers came in to plug the jukebox with quarters.

"They said something about someone getting murdered in his apartment and a trail of blood. They interviewed some old lady who said she was his neighbor."

Will nodded. "That'd be Mrs. Richey. A nosy old bitch, the way Billy puts it."

"She said something about Billy having wild parties and boys up to his apartment."

Will shrugged, studying the grain of the wood on the bar top. "Want some more cherries, little man?" Carl Jr. had a sticky red circle around his mouth, like a clown's mouth. The three-year-old nodded gravely.

"Oh my God, Will, what are you feeding him?" Candy was horrified.

"Just these little candied cherries. It's fruit. Fruit's good for kids."

Candy hoisted the boy onto her hip, wiping his hands with a cocktail napkin as she spoke.

"If you see Billy, or he calls you, you tell him to call me. I don't believe a word of this, and if he needs help, you can be damn sure he'll find it from me!"

She stormed out the door. Will shook his head, absently eating the cherries the boy had left behind. Why, he wondered, did so many good women have such enormous blind spots when it came to men?

As the days went by, the weather grew increasingly oppressive. The temperature climbed into the 90s and stayed there. Will missed the sight of Billy and Candy side by side at the bar, teasing each other about who worked harder. Nearly two weeks after Billy disappeared, Candy stormed into the Anchor again, this time waving a copy of the *Daily Press* over her head.

"They found his truck," she announced. "Last week. They didn't even tell us."

"It's not like we're family or anything, Candy," Will said. "You wanna draft?"

"Sure, gimme a Lite. But that makes it worse."

"What do you mean? You gonna stop drinking?" He set the beer in front of her.

"No, dummy, it's worse that they found his truck." She took a sip, then centered the mug carefully on its paper coaster, avoiding eye contact with Will. "I'm afraid he's not coming back."

Will nodded and sat on the stool next to the cash register. "I know what you mean. At least when they were saying he did it, we knew he was okay."

27

"They mention the vampire thing in here, too," Candy said. "I didn't believe him when he told us that. Did you?"

"You wouldn't believe some of the stories I hear, Candy." Will jumped up and began to polish imaginary spots off the bar. "How's Carl Jr.? You hear from his dad?"

"Oh, that no-good piece of trash." Candy set her beer down crossly. "He sent me two months' back support and promised more, but he didn't even call me back yesterday."

"You deserve better, Candy."

"I know, Will." She examined her nails closely. "I know."

Three days later, Candy was back. As soon as she saw Will, she started sobbing. Wordlessly, she handed him the Friday edition of the *Daily Press*.

"Friend Charged in Murder of Man," Will read. His hands shaking slightly, he reached under the bar for his personal bottle of Scotch. He poured a couple of ounces into two glasses and pushed one over to Candy. He downed his shot and continued to read.

"It says this guy is only 5'4" and 120 pounds." Will started to pour himself another shot, but changed his mind.

"How could a little shrimp like that hurt Billy?" Candy's mascara had migrated below her eyes, reminding Will of the clown-face mouth on her son a few weeks before.

Will just shrugged and bent over the newspaper account. "He loaned the guy money. Says he bought him a car."

"That's our Billy, isn't it?" Candy dabbed at her face with a napkin, and Will wondered if he should tell her not to bother.

"Did you ever see that Wainwright guy in here with him, Will?"

Will shook his head. "But I wouldn't have. The guy's only twenty. He's not old enough to drink."

"Well I can't stand this." Candy stood up, abandoning all efforts to repair her makeup.

"What are you gonna do, Candy?" Will eyed her cautiously. Sometimes she was unpredictable.

"I want some answers."

Will watched as she marched over to the phone next to the restroom, scrambling in the bottom of her purse for quarters. She stood with the receiver at her ear for some time, obviously on hold, before Will took her a draft.

"Who are you calling?" he mouthed.

"The police." She took a sip. "Thanks. I've been on hold forever. Civil servants my ass."

Will was fascinated. "What are you gonna ask them?"

"I'm gonna ask 'em why this guy, this Wainwright, did it." She stared at Will like this was a perfectly obvious question.

Will went back to the bar. People are such amazing creatures, he thought and reread the article. He tried not to think about the body parts they'd found at the apartment, but he wondered what would become of Billy's Confederate flag and the cherished ceremonial swords.

"What do you care who I am?" Candy shrieked. "I'm a friend, damn it, and I have to know why this happened!" She slammed the phone down so hard the machine gave a little apologetic ring in response.

"Be careful, Candy. It says here they may make more arrests."

She glared at Will, and he wondered if he'd gone too far. Then she relented and patted his hand. "I'll tell you what I find out," she promised. "I know Billy is a good friend of yours, too." She slid off the bar stool and slipped her purse strap over her shoulder.

"Where are you going, Candy?" Something told Will she wasn't headed home for a peaceful night in front of the tube.

"The jail, of course."

She tossed her head and cruised out into the oppressive summer heat.

At the County Jail, Candy let Carl Jr. bounce up and down on her hip as she coaxed the officials. "Look, I'm just in town for the day, my bus ticket expires, I've got to talk to my husband."

Carl Jr. let out a wail. "I want my dadddeeee!"

She looked at him, concealing her surprise. "It's okay, honey, the nice man here will let us see your daddy."

29

"Just for a minute, lady." He pressed a button on the intercom and within ten minutes, Candy was face to face with Jeffrey Wainwright.

"Who the hell are you?" he snarled. "I've never seen your ugly ass before."

"The question is, who the hell are you?" Candy pushed her face close to the glass partition. Her eyes got narrow and mean. "Did you kill my Billy?"

The skinny young man's whole frame shook with laughter. "Whoever you are, you were never Billy's," he snickered. "You didn't know him very well."

"He was my friend." Candy sat up straight. "Why did you kill him?"

"I want my daddeee!" Carl Jr. wailed again. Jeff looked from Candy to the boy and back again, confused.

"You tell me!" she hissed at him, tapping on the glass with long, menacing fingernails.

"I didn't mean to." Jeff was scared and momentarily looked like a little boy himself. "I got carried away."

Candy stood up so suddenly her chair tilted over backwards, hitting the floor with a sound like a shot.

"You bastard!" she screamed. "The only nice guy I knew and you killed him!"

The guard in the corner of the room had been dozing on his feet. Now he looked up and headed over, hand on his billy stick. "Calm down, ma'am," he said, bored. Scenes like this were not uncommon.

Carl Jr. looked from his crying mama to the guard, and then to the cowering man behind the glass. "Asshole," he commented and popped his thumb in his mouth.

Later, Will listened to this story open-mouthed. This woman has more balls than a Marine Squad, he thought, and she doesn't even know it.

She polished off her beer and gathered up her purse to go pick up Carl Jr. "I don't believe in vampires any more, Will." She spoke sadly. "But I do believe in evil."

GOTCHA!

aGrange, Georgia, is a typical small Southern town. There are about 500 families, a small college with several hundred students, wide, tree-lined streets, a solid brick courthouse built in the late 1880s, and a once-grand residential section, slightly shabby now.

Only the cemetery in LaGrange is densely populated, with markers dating as far back as the American Revolution. From the road, you can see the tall spires of Confederate memorials, some gracefully draped with stone shawls, tassels sprawling across the wintry gray stone. Some families have stone crypts, ornate granite houses to shelter their beloved dead. Mostly, it's row after row of traditional rectangular markers, a mute testimony to the grief that haunts generation after generation of families. Mothers, infants, fathers, sons, often taken suddenly, without the cold comfort of a simple explanation.

Most of what you see in LaGrange today will remind you of the past. A more gracious time, when a horse's gallop was a speed unnecessary except in the most dire of emergencies. A time when dense heat and humidity was untouched by modern technology, making languid afternoons and oppressive, long nights as inescapable as death itself. In spite of the heat of the day, many found it preferable to the tyranny of the sleepless nights spent in uneasy anticipation of attack.

But there is something stalking LaGrange even now, something impervious to the most modern technology, something that carelessly shrugs off the most archaic of remedies. Every evening, as the shadows grow longer and the night advances, the citizens of LaGrange prepare themselves for the long siege to come, as people have prepared themselves for centuries. With windows tightly closed, talismans in hand, fragrant charms nearby, they await, with a growing sense of disquiet, a merciless onslaught.

When full darkness shrouds the old streets of LaGrange, a creature rises slowly from its daily resting place. Stretching his wings, with delicious anticipation, the creature takes flight, barely hovering over the old brick roads now sheathed in crumbling asphalt. Through the branches of the ancient oaks he wings his way, eagerly seeking the home of his first victim. An antebellum mansion clothed in ragged strips of paint, still genteel, with a tattered petticoat of overgrown azaleas huddled around her porch is his intended destination.

With mounting frustration, he circles the house, first the ground floor and then the second story, seeking a slightly cracked window, a crevice, any way in. Although he would prefer an invitation, he does not expect one, and so an unguarded entrance way is his only hope.

The creature finds no access to the shabby house, and its occupants sleep on, unaware of how close they came to his bloody kiss. His hunger builds as he casts about for another suitable victim.

Farther down the street, he spots a house with a single light burning in an upstairs window. An insomniac. Perhaps, with a little luck, someone who might turn to an open window hoping for the hint of a breeze to stir the sullen summer air. The creature speeds through the night, his powerful wings barely making a sound. Again he circles the house methodically, and this time is rewarded by a bathroom window opened the merest crack. With diabolical ease, he slips inside and searches the hallways and rooms for the evening's first succulent taste of blood.

He reaches what seems to be the only inhabited room. The one whose light beckoned him from blocks away. As he crosses the threshold, all his senses are assailed, pummeled, by an unmistakable odor that fills the room and threatens to overcome him, leaving him senseless and vulnerable on the floor. Reeling, raging with disappointment and hunger, he flees the room and escapes into the night.

Again he hunts, flying through the streets and alleyways of LaGrange, seeking an unprotected victim, an unwary householder. If need be, he will even attack a dog for the essential liquid his body demands, but it is still too early in the evening to consider that less appealing option. Dog's blood simply doesn't have the richness, the savor that he craves.

One might think that this horror stalking LaGrange is particular to that small town. But every night, there are countless numbers of these creatures, searching for the life-giving elixir. No one in any town or city or lonely farmstead is immune to the threat these creatures bring. Just because we do not always see them does not mean they do not exist.

There is a power in nature that destroys homes and crops, uproots ancient trees, and carries away everything in its path. You can't deny its existence just because you haven't seen it. Who has ever seen the wind?

As the night wanes and Earth's orbit mercifully inches LaGrange closer to the saving daybreak, the creature's rage and hunger heightens to a silent scream within his body. Just as he is about to mount a desperate attack on the first victim he sees, regardless of the threat to his safety, he discovers a tiny tear on a screen that guards an open window. Triumphant, he soars through the darkened house, as yet unstained by the coming dawn.

He finds his victim and falls to her neck in greedy lust. As he drinks and the blood courses through his body, he feels not only refreshed, but unconquerable, inviolate. In taking, he becomes one with her strength and beauty.

She stirs and groans, but the creature is so enraptured with his feast that he ignores the danger. He sucks on, oblivious.

Half asleep, his victim reaches up, slaps her neck, and sits up, barely conscious. The creature lies on the floor, his translucent wings barely fluttering, dying.

"Damn mosquitoes," she says, and rolls over to return to her dreams. A smudge of blood on her neck and a small round swelling are all that remain to remind her of the creature's nocturnal plunder. His tiny carcass, with its needlelike mouth and hair-thin legs, is blown by an errant breeze to oblivion among the dust clots beneath her bed.

Little Man

he opium coursed through his blood like blue fire, rich and explosive. He remembered, as if from a great distance, the sinuous arm of the hookah, with its bright, glittering mouthpiece. He recalled seeing bubbles float lazily to the surface of the water inside the elaborate pipe, which squatted on the floor like a malevolent child. He recalled the soft touch of velvet and the whispered endearments of the mulatto girl beside him.

The little man's hand reached out to stroke her chicory colored skin and recoiled at the touch of unyielding cold stone. He felt a spatter of something wet and reeking splashed onto his cheek. He heard the clip-clop of a horse making its way along the cobblestone streets. He knew he was in New Orleans, and he struggled to remember more.

He was splashed again, this time by a bucketful of slops thrown from a second-story window. He shook himself, like a dog, and struggled to his knees. Raucous laughter floated down from above.

"Whatcher drinkin', little man?" jeered the voice, but he ignored it with the curious kind of dignity sometimes found in drunkards, cats, and very young children.

Crawling along the street, using the low curb as a guide, he reached the corner. Hand over hand, painfully, he pulled himself up on a lamp-post. He squinted, but the street signs were too far above him to resolve into recognizable letters, so he hazarded a guess and turned right. He hoped that was the right direction.

The world around him straggled off into a gray shroud a mere three feet in every direction. Slowly he began to realize that this was not solely an effect of the drug. His hands groped around above his nose. Nothing there. His thick, indispensable eyeglasses were lost in the muck back there at whatever street that was. Or maybe lying smashed and useless on the floor of the opium den. He squinted but could not tell where the sun was. He had no way of knowing how long he'd been unconscious. He shrugged and staggered a few feet more.

His eyes might be worthless, but his hearing was good. Ahead of him, he heard a pulsing rhythm that seemed to stir the narcotic in his blood, summoning a faint echo of the euphoria that had gripped him hours earlier. He moved closer. The drumbeats seemed to peel away essential layers of his soul, exposing a gaping hunger in the very center of his gut. It was an oddly pleasant sensation.

Straining to see ahead, he tripped over a curbstone and fell headlong into an overgrown azalea. Now the driving rhythms were closer still, and he felt his heart begin to contract and expand in accord with the compelling beat. Cautiously, he spread the branches of the shrub and peered out.

Dancing brown figures whirled so close he could have touched the vibrant golds, greens, oranges, and blues of their skirts. Some had their hair wrapped in the tignon, mark of the free colored woman, while others let their hair swing loose. Men, too, swirled by the little man in his hiding spot, their torsos slick with sweat and their feet pounding, slapping, punctuating the cadence of the drums.

The man felt a force at the center of this circle so commanding it drew him out of the bush. As he slithered forward, too weakened to walk or even crawl on hands and knees, the dancers slowed. The drums tailed off one by one. But the tall woman at the center of the circle, draped with the thick, fleshy coils of a snake, continued to clap her hands in time to her own dreams and move her hips from side to side as she stared at the little man who had appeared at her summoning.

"A sign from Zombi!" she roared.

The little man looked up into the face of a mocha angel. And passed out again.

When he awoke, a hand with fingers like brittle sticks was gently wiping his face. He blinked once, twice, trying to bring the face into focus, into memory. But the face, wizened and brown like fruit left too long in the sun, with bright brown eyes like points of amber, was nothing like he remembered. He sat up.

"You're not her," he stammered.

The woman shrieked with laughter.

"No, laws, no, I ain't. You think she lay hands on the likes of you?" Her hands lost some of their gentleness.

The door creaked open, and the man squinted at the shape approaching the bed. It was a tall, commanding presence. As it stood over him, the features, skin tones, and gestures coalesced into the angel of his memory.

"Who are you?"

She made a low sound in her throat. Not quite a laugh.

"No, little man, the question is, who are you?"

He was quite a little man. Just over five feet tall and oddly misshapen. His arms were too long for his torso, and the size of his head overpowered everything. Except, of course, for his one remaining eye. It was huge, blue, almost always stretched open wide, as if in surprise, and virtually useless, especially without his glasses. He could make out shapes within eight feet, but to distinguish individual faces, they had to be within twelve inches of his nose. He could not read for long periods of time, because his eye quickly tired of the print held just a few inches away.

He shook his head, as if to clear it.

"I don't know."

Her laugh, when it came, was delightful. Low, and rich, and satisfying. An Easter feast after Lenten fast.

He blushed, then was amazed to realize what that warm sensation was. He had not had a woman make him feel this way since. . . well, since he could remember.

"The last thing I remember was being in an opium den," he said. This provoked knowing cackles from the old crone who'd first attended him.

"But here, look in my wallet. . ." He reached for his back pocket and then realized his pants were gone. The two women were now convulsed with laughter.

When she caught her breath, the angel spoke. "You surely didn't expect to leave the opium den with your wallet, did you? Where are you from?"

"Not New Orleans," he said, with a deep-seated certainty.

"Go get him some broth, Kitty." The tall woman pulled a shawl around her shoulders and settled on a stool next to the bed.

"I shall call you. . ." She thought for a moment. Then her eyes lit up with mischief. "I shall call you Jacob. Although by the looks of you, you haven't won any wrestling matches in a while."

"But these little legs were made for climbing ladders."

"Whatever's wrong with you, your wits aren't much addled." She looked at him sharply. "You truly don't know who I am?"

"No." His simple answer had the ring of truth.

She rose and left the room, ordering Kitty to care for him well.

He slept the rest of that day, and his brief waking moments had an unreal mistiness that he could attribute to the after-effects of the drug or to his lack of vision. But that night, when the noise of carriages passing on the street outside had dwindled, he awoke with a startling clarity.

He slipped out of the bed and searched the small room swiftly for his clothes. Looking for clothes in a dark room was a familiar exercise, he thought wryly, and that doesn't bode well for my character, whoever I may be. He found his pants; they had been washed, and there was nothing in the pockets.

He crept out of the room and found himself in a narrow hall. It was quite dark, but that was no hindrance. Placing one hand on the wall, he moved quietly toward the light and sound at the end of the hall. The sound was low, susurrant, like waves washing up on shore or the sound of a light wind stirring leaves in the spring. It was accentuated by a slow, heavy rhythm, so deep and throbbing that the man at first mistook it for his own heartbeat.

He reached a set of doors and crossed the threshold hesitantly. The upper veranda was deserted. Below, in the courtyard, foliage twisted and climbed in a riotous celebration of rampant greens. In the center were perhaps a dozen people, lit by a bonfire whose leaping flames seemed to mock, in shades of reds and yellows, the exuberant garden.

He realized what the low, hissing sound was. They were chanting.

"Marie Laveau, Queen of the Voodoo. Marie Laveau, Queen of the Voodoo. Marie Laveau, Queen of the Voodoo." The drumbeats highlighted the chant, anchoring the yearning sound to the cold, fertile earth.

The man was uncomprehending until a familiar form, regal and commanding, entered the garden. The chanting stopped, but the drums continued. Marie Laveau raised her arms high above her head, and the ceremony began.

The little man could not see the particulars of the ritual. He could not make out faces or see what objects different people held in their hands. He couldn't hear the whispered supplications, and he could only guess that the writhing, thick rope around the neck and shoulders of the queen was the same massive snake he'd seen at the earlier ceremony. But the insistent pounding, pounding of the drums reached him up in his sanctuary, and after a while, he fell under its spell. Mesmerized, he swayed to the pulse, incorporating it into his own.

A scream woke him from his trance. He strained to see over the railing, into the courtyard. Marie Laveau held a form in her strong hands that struggled wildly, squawking in terror. As he watched, she slit its neck expertly and held the carcass over her face to catch the spouting blood between her eager lips.

"Come, Zombi, come Zombi, come Zombi."

An insistent chant began to rise again from the courtyard. Marie fell to the ground, twitching. The man's temples began to pound. Marie convulsed. He collapsed.

When he awoke, he was in the bed in the small front room. Kitty was fussing with some dishes on a tray and turned when she heard a sound.

"You," she grunted and left.

Marie glided in a few moments later and seated herself on the stool by the bed.

"You know who I am." It was not a question.

He nodded.

"What did you see?"

He gestured to his eye. "Very little."

"Uninvited guests meet untimely deaths."

"You would kill me for witnessing the sacrifice of a chicken?"

Her eyes searched his eye for a long, long time. Then she nodded and rose.

"Be careful," she said. She shut the door softly behind her.

Late that night, after he had a solitary dinner in his room, Kitty bustled in with a bottle and a glass.

"From the lady," she said. "I 'spect you're bored."

He nodded and stared at the bottle for a while after Kitty left. He wondered what kind of evil genies might come spiraling out if he uncorked it. Shrugging, he poured himself a drink anyway and upended the glass. Nothing evil came. Just a pleasant, familiar stupor.

The drums woke him again that night or maybe it was early morning. But his limbs were too heavy, the feather mattress too enfolding for him to get up and investigate. He lay in bed, allowed his pulse to synchronize with the tempo of the drums, and drifted back to sleep.

When he awoke and rolled over to leave the bed, a dull throbbing in his neck made him stop momentarily. He reached up, and his fingers found a short scab, no longer than two inches. He dismissed it as one more relic of the opium den.

After breakfast, he sat in the sun on the back veranda, oddly content, like a cat, to sit and do nothing. Marie visited him for a while. She would not answer his questions about voodoo, but would occasionally share with him observations about New Orleans and its people.

"I used to dress women's hair, you know," she said, idly twisting a lock of her own as she spoke.

"So you became an observer of human nature. Not the nicer side, I imagine."

He felt her eyes on him like a burning brand.

"Negroes seldom see the nicer side of human nature." She pushed up and out of her chair. "Sometimes you try my patience, Jacob."

He thought she was leaving, but she returned in a moment with a bottle and two glasses.

"Wine," she said shortly. "I make it myself." They shared a glass or two in companionable silence, and then Marie went back to her daily life. The alcohol made the man drowsy, and he napped off and on all afternoon.

He did not drink after dinner. Perhaps that was the explanation for his wide-awake state after midnight, or perhaps it was the sterile light of the moon, pouring in through cracks in the shutters. He lay still and listened to the rhythms from the courtyard for what seemed to be hours before he succumbed to the temptation, uncurled himself, and stole down the hallway like a misshapen ghost.

In the courtyard, the drums had worked themselves into a frenzy. It did not take him long to pick out the shape of Marie; he had become familiar with her gestures, her ways of moving. This time, the cries of her followers were more guttural, more painful. The snake refused to stay put around Marie's shoulders and writhed hugely on the bricks of the terrace beside her. It seemed inevitable that her constantly moving feet would trample the serpent, but miraculously, the two never came into contact. There was a tension in the air that had been lacking during the other rituals. The little man cursed his eyesight for the millionth time.

Marie lifted a struggling shape above her head. The man's head ached and his eye teared with the effort of trying to make out the scene below. The drums reached a crescendo. The chanting rose and fell, rose, and then rose again. The sacrifice shrieked once, a chilling cry. Marie drank and smeared the ritual blood on the hands and faces of the dancers around her.

The man felt weak. Frightened. He crept back to his bed and waited for morning.

Kitty brought him steaming coffee and opened the shutters without speaking.

"May I have a paper?"

She shuffled off and returned with the *Daily Picayune*. Something about the smudged ink stirred the man's memory, but it fled as soon as he tried to pin it down. He thanked her and turned to the inside page. The steamer *Strassburg* was leaving on the 26th for Havana. Maybe that's what he needed, to escape this damnable city. This maddening woman. His hand, without thought, wandered up to his neck. A second scab had formed just below the first.

Kitty came back in and without a word collected the dishes and the newspaper.

Marie came to him after breakfast.

"Am I a prisoner?"

She made an amused sound in her throat. "Do you want to be?"

He collapsed back onto the bed.

"I'm sorry. You've treated me very well. I don't understand why I seem to be getting weaker, after so much rest."

Her smile was so faint he almost missed it. "Opium is a very potent substance."

"What is happening to me?"

Her hand reached to smooth his brow. "Poor Jacob."

He drank that night, after dinner, and stuffed his head beneath a pillow to block out the sound of the drums and the equally insistent moonlight. But when he woke, the pulsing sound penetrated the pillow's frail defenses. He felt drawn to witness again the ritual that bound Marie and her followers in faith.

This time, he crept down the stairs. The house seemed deserted, and he worked his way stealthily to the doors leading out to the courtyard. From his screen of wisteria vines, the drummers were a scant three feet away.

One of them turned suddenly, and Jacob drew back, afraid of discovery. Behind him, unseen in the shadows, lay a slight figure, bound with ropes. He stumbled over it, they both bleated in terror, and the ceremony ended in shouts of betrayal.

The little man had a vague memory of brown, ebony, hazel, and tan faces surrounding him as he lay on the ground.

"Kill him," one said, and he thought he recognized the voice of Kitty.

"No," said another. "He will remember nothing." The words came from the lips of an angel.

The man's nose picked up the rank scent of goat, and he turned his head. Beside him struggled a young kid, its horns just buds still, with a gleaming white coat.

Morning came, and his head was once again pillowed on cobblestones. A wagon creaked by, and the mule's hooves threw up a clod of mud and manure into the man's wide staring eye.

"Here, what's this?"

The wagon driver was a rag picker. He thought the little man was a bundle of rags cast off by an industrious housewife.

He took the man to Charity Hospital. There they cared for him and waited for his memory to return. Once he had regained his strength, they found odd jobs for him to do. Someone gave him a pen and paper, to help patients write letters home, and the weight of the pen in his hand brought a flood of memories rushing back.

"I'm a journalist," he cried, turning the pen wonderingly over and over in his hand. "I'm a writer."

He left the hospital. Years later, he left New Orleans. He only mentioned his strange interlude with Marie Laveau once, in a letter to a friend.

"I lived with a vampire in New Orleans," he wrote.

He was a well-known journalist in the late nineteenth century, although admittedly a bit odd. He traveled all over the world, finally choosing Japan as his home.

But he returned to New Orleans once, many years after his first visit. A bent, crippled old man, with an untamed halo of hair and a single, startlingly blue eye, he wandered through the tombs of St. Louis Cemetery #1. At last he found the simple structure reputed to be the resting place of Marie Laveau's earthly remains.

He placed one tiny, clawlike hand on the side of the tomb and laughed out loud. The wind tore his words from his throat, a ragged cry that lifted above the city like little birds.

"She's not here! Wherever she may be, she's not here!"

INTERVIEW WITH A VAMPIRE OR TWO

impsonville, South Caro-
lina: a town with a past. A prosperous Cherokee village was once situat-
ed near where the present town stands. But in 1761, when the distant
King George III deeded nearly fifteen thousand acres of this languidly
rolling, fertile land to Nathaniel Austin, the Cherokee influence began
to wane. During the Revolutionary War, the Cherokees sided with the
British, so General George Washington sent a detachment to chase the
Native Americans into the Great Smoky Mountains, where they
remained for years. Blood again soaked the earth at the Battle of the
Great Canebrake, near Simpsonville, in 1786.

While the present town doesn't reflect these earliest conflicts, there
are visible signs of tension between old and new. The old town is clustered around the railroad tracks, with fine old houses, nineteenth-centu-
ry storefronts, and quiet residential streets lined with middle-class, older
bungalows. These streets look like your grandma's neighborhood: narrow,
crumbling asphalt roads, steps leading to deep and shadowy front porch-
es flanked by cracked cement planters holding faded plastic flowers.

But this isn't all there is to Simpsonville. If you take the right turns,
you'll find yourself on a road than runs parallel to the interstate. Before
long, you'll forget about the turn-of-the-century charm of old
Simpsonville in the barrage of twentieth-century consumerism that
awaits you here. McDonald's, Comfort Inn, Texaco, K-Mart: they all
scream at you with bright banners and signs tearing upward into the sky.

Near this strip is the new high school, overlooking the freeway, with its back placed squarely toward the old town center.

I am sure the architects intended to make the high school look like a modern, cool place to be. I am sure they had no intention of making it look like a penitentiary. Or perhaps they had teenagers and a subconscious urge to lock them up where they could do no harm. Regardless, the new, multi-million dollar high school looks like a prison: stark gray walls, tall forbidding fences, tiny windows. Around back, a crowd of sullen kids sits outside what must be the lunchroom, with clouds of either steam or cigarette smoke rising from them. A small basketball court packed with leaping, stretching, shouting boys completes the image of a prison.

Surrounding these bits and pieces of urban America are the kinds of subdivisions so studied in their reach for individuality that they all begin to look alike, in spite of the odd turns of the streets, the "custom" doors, the whimsically shaped windows. Each house is clad in plastic molded to look like wood, and each has at least a double garage. The subdivisions and their streets are cleverly named, to evoke memories of a more noble lifestyle or perhaps to hint at a time when servants were affordable and Queen Victoria ruled. Here live the more well-to-do residents of Simpsonville, many of whom work in nearby Greenville but chose to reside in the simpler, less crime-ridden, small town.

Here also lives a vampire, or as close to the species as I would care to know. She lives with her parents while she attends college, and works at K-Mart between classes. I will call her Lauren. She speaks with a Southern drawl, stretching out her vowels like taffy. It has a country twang to it, reminiscent of the mountains that are only an hour's drive away. Her voice is pitched low, either deliberately or as a natural consequence of her cigarette habit—I can't tell which.

I met Lauren in Waffle House one evening in late fall. She has two close friends, one of whom is also a vampire (I'll call him Steve), and one who is not (I'll call him Rick). All three are in their early twenties. I interviewed all of them the next day at a coffee bar. The following is a synopsis of both interviews. During the initial interview and the second one, both Lauren and Steve were visibly nervous and tightly strung.

Their hands shook, and they smoked incessantly. Rick also smoked, but seemed less nervous, understandably so.

KZ: Where were you born?

Lauren: Right here, in Simpsonville. It's a pretty old town. I heard there was an old Indian village near here, and they used to be cannibals or something.

Steve: In Simpsonville.

KZ: Where have you lived since then?

Lauren: I've always lived here.

Steve: Me, too. Unfortunately (he laughs).

KZ: How would you describe your childhood?

Lauren: I had fun, I guess. I didn't have any problems or anything.

Steve: It was pathetic (he laughs again, nervously, and examines his hands). I'm an only child and live out in the middle of nowhere.

Rick: I knew him for two years before his mother would even let him come over to my house.

Lauren: When we started dating, we used to have to sneak him outta the house. Then at Prom Night, he just said, "Look, I'm goin'," and I was sitting there, nervous, while she was looking me over. I had to have him home by nine o'clock.

Rick: He still has to be in by eleven, or she freaks out.

Steve: I think she's half insane, anyhow.

Lauren: She talks to the cat more than she talks to me.

KZ: What vampire tendencies do you have?

Lauren: That's a pretty strange question! I feel weird talking about it (she takes a deep breath). Well, I drink blood.

KZ: When did this tendency first appear?

Lauren: I've always been different. It started when I was in middle school or even sooner. I'd get a cut and stick it in my mouth. You know. I hadn't really thought about it.

Steve: I always had it [the craving]. But up until three or four years ago, I thought it was sick or something. But now, I just do what feels natural.

KZ: What do you think caused these tendencies to appear?

Lauren: I don't know. While I was in middle school, I smoked a lot of pot, and I went to Main Street, and they were talking about it. So I tried it. We were all pretty much out of it. I pestered this guy until he did it. Cut himself. That was the first time.

KZ: What needs do these tendencies satisfy?

Lauren: It's not like an addiction or anything. I don't have to have it. I've read about other people who have to have it. I guess for them it's more psychological.

KZ: Do you think it's an addiction, Steve?

Steve: (Nods.)

KZ: How do you satisfy your desire for blood?

Lauren: I go out a lot, and this may sound strange, but I know a lot of people. Usually I know them. I get them to cut themselves, and then I get it from them.

KZ: How often do you. . .

Lauren: It depends. Last week about twelve times. But it varies. Last week I went out a lot. There are a lot of gothic types that hang out in Greenville, and you get to talking to them and they say, "Yes, I've always wanted to be a vampire," so then you like, take advantage of that and talk to them. If they don't want to, I don't push them into it or anything. I say it jokingly, so if they turn me down, they don't feel weird about me.

Steve: It goes in cycles. About twice a month usually. I've never hunted like she does. Usually I just get it from myself.

KZ: Do you ever worry about AIDS?

Lauren: (She takes a deep pull off her cigarette, stubs it out and immediately lights another.) That's a good question. I've read a lot just finding out how it's spread, but I keep it with a circle of friends that I know. I just don't go with anybody I don't know.

KZ: Have your needs changed over the years?

Lauren: Not really.

Steve: It seems like I want a lot more lately.

KZ: How do you feel after satisfying these needs?

Lauren: (She laughs nervously.) Well, I guess it's like after a good meal, after you eat something you really like. It's different than sex. It doesn't have anything to do with sex. It's not really like eating. It's hard to describe. It's a mental thing.

Steve: Like being high. I get a rush off of it. It's better than smoking pot. It feels. . .like an orgasm. Before I drink, I feel out of control. Sort of edgy, jittery.

KZ: Have you told anyone? How did they react?

Lauren: I have a girlfriend who knows, but she doesn't mind. I haven't told very many people. Everybody's always thought I was strange.

KZ: Were you influenced by anyone in regard to these tendencies?

Lauren: I didn't get around to reading *Dracula* until last year.

Steve: I've read a fair number of books but not till after I started, you know, drinking blood.

KZ: How do you feel about your vampire tendencies?

Lauren: They don't bother me. It has no big effect on my life.

Steve: If it's what you want to do, go ahead and do it. I figure one day I'll start getting it from other people. The same way she does.

KZ: What, if any, religious influences did you have as a child?

Lauren: I used to go to church every Sunday, but the church started getting hard on me. When they started growing and getting a lot of new members, they didn't like the way I dressed, wouldn't let me read [to the congregation from the Bible during services] and all. So I quit going. I keep it [blood drinking] pretty separate. I am a Christian. I don't see any conflict between my religious beliefs and drinking blood. I may be wrong, but I don't.

Steve: My parents are real religious.

Lauren: Too religious.

Rick: I believe in God, and I'm religious, but I don't believe you should go and shove people's noses in it. I think church is just a place to go to show off your fancy new clothes. I don't wanna be a part of that.

KZ: What about all the vampire stereotypes? Crosses, garlic, and all that?

Lauren: I wear crosses, I eat lots of garlic, I'm around in the daylight. I do have insomnia. I've read about people who try to live totally at night, but that's pretty impossible. Not that many jobs you can find just at night.

KZ: How is your life different because of these tendencies?

Lauren: I don't think it's anything bad. I think I'd still hang out with the same people and everything.

Steve: It's a lot more secretive. I keep a lot more stuff from my parents now.

KZ: Are you happy?

Steve: With my lifestyle? Yeah, I'm happy with that.

KZ: Has anyone in your family had these tendencies?

Lauren: I don't know, honestly. My sister is kind of weird, but I have no idea what she does.

KZ: Do you ever wish you weren't a vampire?

Lauren: No.

(Steve did not respond)

KZ: Do you think you're immortal?

Lauren: (Laughs.) I don't know. I don't think I wanna try. I guess for lack of a better word, I'd say I'm a vampire. But I don't have superhuman strength or anything. But I've had dreams that kinda told the future. And I've read Tarot cards to people. It seems I may have some psychic stuff, but I wouldn't put any money on it. But I don't think it's related to me being a vampire.

KZ: Have you seen *Interview With A Vampire*? What did you think?

Lauren: I've seen it eight times. My sister saw it, and now she wants to get caps on her teeth. You know, with fangs. She's saving up her money now.

Steve: I've seen it three times.

KZ: What would your family think if they knew?

Lauren: My mom would have a fit. My dad would vomit. He has such a weak stomach. I'd never tell them.

Steve: My parents would probably kick me out of the house. They're Holy Rollers.

KZ: What do you see in your future?

Lauren: I'd like to get married someday. But I don't know why I'd ever stop, you know, drinking it. I want to move out of my parents' house, and I don't want to live in a trailer like most people around here.

Steve: I guess I'll be a freelance writer. Anything to get out of here. I'd like to get married. But she'd have to accept me the way I am. Love me, love my practices.

Rick: I'd like to get out of Simpsonville too.

KZ: Do you think there's a relationship between being a vampire and cannibalism?

Lauren: Well, yeah, actually, probably. Because, well, blood is really, well, what you're doing is borderline. But I've never had any desire, you know. I've read a lot about people like Jeffrey Dahmer, and he was really gone. What he did was uncalled for. I'd never kill anybody.

KZ: How is Satanism related to what you do?

Rick: I've always loved horror movies and ancient weapons, but I'm not into Satanism.

Lauren: There are people in Simpsonville into that, but we're not.

KZ: Have you ever drunk animal blood?

Lauren: No. Well, I always eat rare steak.

Steve: Just once. It turned my stomach. I'll never do that again.

KZ: Do you all feed off each other?

Steve: Uh, twice? (He looks to Lauren for confirmation.)

Lauren: More than that. (She giggles.)

KZ: Is it different with friends? Better?

Steve: Yeah.

Lauren: (Nods.)

KZ: How about Rick? Has he ever, do you say, 'donated' for you?

Lauren: (Laughs.)

Steve: He's too squeamish.

Rick: I'm not too squeamish. Cutting and stuff don't bother me, but I ain't lettin' nobody bite me.

KZ: Do you prefer to bite your donors?

Steve: I'd rather let them cut themselves. I don't want anybody to get hurt. If they wanted me to bite 'em, I guess I wouldn't object to it.

KZ: Does this strike you as bizarre, Rick?

Rick: No. The one thing I thought was weird was when you asked me if I'd ever given my blood for Steve. I just can't see guys giving blood to other guys or a girl using another girl. It just wouldn't seem right.

KZ: Lauren, have you ever gotten blood from another girl?

Lauren: (Giggles.) No. It's always been guys.

KZ: Is there anything you think I ought to know?

Rick: Steve and me, we're both, always, well, we've never really been happy. No matter what we do, or how well we plan it, somebody's gonna come along and hassle us. Me 'n' him, other than the blood drinking, we're a whole lot alike.

KZ: Are you evil?

Steve: (Pauses and thinks for a long time.) Well, I think apathy is evil. And I am apathetic. So, yes, I guess I am evil.

TEXAS TERROR

ome vampires cannot be
put to rest. And although they may not suck their victims' blood, they
still have the capacity to drain away the spirit, the will to live. And that
may be the cruelest appetite of all: a vampire's hunger for human joy.

Tyler, Texas was about as typical a small city as you could find in
1965. Elizabeth Street, lined with pleasant trees and modest, unexcep-
tional ranch-style houses, was so ordinary no one would have given it a
second glance. But one house had more than its fair share of occupants.

"What are you doing, Andy?" Howard Beaird set down the box of
linens before he reached the bathroom because the sight of his youngest
child, thirteen-year-old Andy, filled him with inexplicable dread. The
boy sat quite still—unusually still for a normally restless teenager—in the
middle of his empty room.

"I don't know why we came here, Dad," the boy said softly. "I don't
want to be here."

Howard sighed. "We've been over this already, Andy," he said, trying—and failing—to sound patient. "Since your mother got out of the
hospital, I thought it would help to move somewhere new. We have to
do what's best for her. I know you miss your friends, but you'll make new
ones." He stood up and brushed some dust clots off the knees of his slacks.
"Now, come on. I need your help."

Howard and Andy worked like dogs over the next few days, moving,
unpacking, arranging, and cleaning. "Why won't Mom help?" Andy whispered to his dad, more than once. "She just sits there and stares off into space."

51

Howard would sigh. That had become his most frequent form of communication these days. "Give her time, Andy," he'd say. And he'd fix toast and soup for dinner, which was always a solemn occasion unmarked by casual conversation. During meals, Andy watched his mother, hoping to see signs of the laughing, lively friend she'd been before her tenure in the state mental hospital. Howard watched his son.

After little more than a month, Johnnie began to fuss. "They're watching me, Howard," she whined. "They're all over the house. I feel their eyes on me."

From the corner where he sat with an unopened math book in his lap, Andy listened intently.

"There's nobody here but us, Johnnie," his dad replied. But she continued to complain, and soon, Howard just tuned her out. He went through his routine numbly, going to work, coming home, cooking, cleaning, checking Andy's homework occasionally, and then going out to his workshop to make a little extra money because he never could quite seem to make ends meet.

"Dad."

Howard turned to see his son at the door to the workshop one night in midsummer.

"She started a fire in the bathroom." Andy was pale and out of breath, and Howard threw down his tools and ran to the narrow tiled room sandwiched between the bedrooms. A wad of paper towels burned merrily next to the toilet. Howard stomped it out, wondering grimly how long he could manage to keep Johnnie at home.

Andy and Howard began to share a room so Johnnie could have her privacy. Howard would kick off his house slippers, tell his son good night, and crawl beneath the covers to wait for sleep and another day. The night of the fire, as soon as he turned out the bedside lamp, the bed was besieged by a storm of June bugs.

"What the hell?" Howard shouted and turned on the lamp. The bugs immediately stopped flying. But the bed and the floor around it was littered with the creatures.

"Dad, they're all dead." Andy picked one up and turned to his father, looking for an explanation.

Howard could only shrug. "Maybe the bugs are coming in through a hole in the screen, Andy," he said, although that sounded lame even to him. "Let's get these cleaned up and go to sleep, okay?" They swept up the bugs and turned out the light once more.

Again a torrent of brown, dried bugs bombarded the bed from the ceiling directly overhead. Again Howard turned on the light, which stopped the puzzling deluge. That night, Andy and Howard filled the bathroom trashcan with brittle, dead June bugs, which fell on them over and over each time Howard turned off the light.

"Why don't you leave the light on, Dad?" Andy finally suggested. He tried desperately to sound matter-of-fact about the whole strange episode, but there was a strained note to his voice. This onslaught of bugs was beyond any rational explanation, but there was not much rational about the teenager's life at the moment anyway.

A few days later, Andy came home late from school. He lounged against the door frame to the kitchen, unseen, as his dad talked to his older sister on the phone. "I'm worried about Andy, Amy. You know how lively he was when he was little. Now he doesn't seem to laugh at all, and he doesn't have any friends."

Andy stepped into the room. "How can I have any friends, Dad?" he demanded bitterly. "I live in a bug-infested house, and my mom's got bats in her belfry. Who would *want* to be my friend?" He stalked angrily to the bedroom and slammed the door. Events in the house on Elizabeth Street would soon set him even further apart from his peers.

Howard believed that somehow Johnnie was responsible for the storm of June bugs every night. When those bugs turned into little wood lice, hard, pellet-like bugs that struck with enough force to sting the skin, he confronted his wife.

"You'll have to leave, Johnnie," he said. "Go stay with your sister for a while. This is driving me crazy, and it's bad for Andy too." Johnnie, still insisting that she was being watched, agreed to leave. The house was just as oppressive to her as her presence was to her husband.

"Now, at last we'll have some peace and quiet," Howard thought. He couldn't have been more wrong.

"Put a little more salt in that," commanded a woman's voice from behind his left shoulder as he stirred a can of Campbell's vegetable beef soup. Howard whirled around, expecting to see an intruder in his kitchen. But no one was there.

A few minutes later Andy came into the kitchen. "Dad, some woman just told me to get started on my spelling homework," he said. "But when I turned around, there was nobody there."

"Well, I guess you'd better do what she says, son," Howard said, trying to laugh. But the instructions, comments, and advice increased daily, until finally Howard demanded, "Who are you?"

A scrap of paper materialized in the air and floated lazily into his hand. "Mrs. Elliot," read the note.

"But you're dead," breathed Howard. "You're Lannie Elliot's mother, and you died of cancer in 1955."

"Mrs. Snow and I will take care of you," the voice said.

"But really, we're here for the boy," said a second voice. "He'll really need us soon."

Andy appeared in the kitchen doorway one night as Howard shaped hamburger patties and slapped them into a skillet. "Dad," he announced, "Mrs. Elliot says you need to get me a cat."

"The boy's lonely without his mother," a voice from the living room said. "He needs a pet to keep him company after school."

When Howard brought home a small white kitten the next day, Andy was overjoyed. Mrs. Elliot and a new voice, Mr. Gree, told him just how to care for it. The boy lavished affection on the creature, giving it all the love his mother no longer responded to.

Incredibly enough, Andy and Howard seemed to adjust to these disembodied voices telling them not to put too much starch on their shirts or to cook the roast a little longer. It was no more strange than bugs flying through the night and certainly a good deal more benign.

Then the visits from Henry Anglin started.

Howard was working late in his workshop one night when he looked up to see a can of bug spray suspended in midair. A choking cloud of white vapor quickly filled the small space, and Howard struggled to get the door open, finally staggering outside and sucking in great whooping gasps of fresh air. "What was that?" he wondered aloud, and a note materialized in the clear night air above him.

"Watch out," it said. "Henry Anglin is a killer."

That night the torrent of insects bombarding the bed seemed a little less intense. Over the next few nights, the flying bugs gradually tapered off, and life looked like it might return to a state more closely resembling normalcy.

Howard was enjoying his second night of slumber without bugs when he felt something slither along the skin of his hand. Half-asleep, his first thought was that Andy had reached out in his sleep. Some primeval sense made him grope for the lamp switch on the table near his bed.

As the light illuminated his flesh, his stomach heaved with revulsion.

"Oh, my God," he cried and shook himself violently in a grotesque parody of a dance. Thick, rubbery slugs were attached to his hands, torso, and legs, leaving a glistening trail of sticky slime as they moved across his skin. Some were only a half-inch long, but some were as big as a Vienna sausage. Standing over the toilet, he picked them off and dropped them in to disappear in a storm of water. Andy, too, was infested with slugs, and Howard wanted desperately to join him in his frantic sobbing as they pulled the gruesome creatures loose from their flesh.

Every night, Howard and Andy found slugs in their bed. Sometimes just three or four, sometimes dozens. Andy suggested putting salt around the bed, but neither that nor anything else worked. One morning after they had been besieged by slugs and bugs, Andy came to his dad holding a crumpled white form in his arms.

He struggled to hold back his tears. "She died, Dad," he said. "I guess I'll have to bury her, huh?"

Howard gave his son an awkward hug. "I'm sorry, Andy," he said. "I'll get you another cat, I promise."

When Andy came home that afternoon, he found a bar of soap that had been crushed and scattered in the living room. He cleaned it up and wrote a note to his mom at her sister's house in Daingerfield, Texas. Then he settled in to do his homework with the occasional friendly comment from Mrs. Elliot, Mrs. Snow, or Mr. Gree. That night, a mild September evening, Howard was outside hanging clothes on the line when he saw his son's pallid face looming up in the darkness.

"Dad, it's crazy in there," he said, out of breath from his hasty exit. "There are slugs flying through the house and smashing on the walls, and all kinds of bugs flying around. Even though all the lights are on, they just keep coming out of nowhere."

Howard felt like crying. He couldn't escape this insanity. No one in his right mind would believe this story. But he was living it. He and his son were being mercilessly tormented, and there was no way out. He didn't say a word but sat down on the grass and stared up at the stars as he blinked away his tears of frustration and fear. Andy sat down beside him, and they sat without words, waiting for their hell to end.

When they went back inside, the remains of slugs and June bugs, pill bugs and doodle bugs littered every room. They cleaned the kitchen and the bedroom before falling into bed, anticipating the storm of slugs that would come when the lights went out.

Howard brought Andy a Siamese cat the next day. It was vocal and playful, loudly protesting the occasional storms of bugs but delighting in the way the dried corpses skittered across the floor when she batted them with her paws. Just days after the cat came to live with them, Howard got a note from Henry Anglin that chilled him:

I pOisOned
little FOOLS
white kittEn
ShALL i
poisOn The
Jap Cat

He didn't show the note to Andy, but Mrs. Elliot whispered to him that Henry Anglin had killed before.

"He causes automobile wrecks," she hissed. "He switches pills in bottles, and people die from the wrong medicine. You better watch out for Henry Anglin!"

In November, the slugs started flying every night, smashing on the walls and leaving a sickening trail of dark slime as the corpses slid down to the baseboards. The Siamese disappeared, but Howard didn't have the heart to say anything to Andy about her. Andy became more withdrawn, and the two of them sometimes went for days with only three or four words between them. While cleaning up the slugs one afternoon, Howard found a note saying that the bugs would stop on December 29th. He didn't believe it and thought he could hear Henry Anglin's mocking laughter as he crumpled up the note and tossed it on top of the crushed slugs.

"I'm going to get all the locks changed tomorrow, Andy." It was the day before Thanksgiving, and the two of them had made no plans for the holiday. They sat at the table eating soup and toast.

Andy laughed, but it was a humorless sound. "You think that will make it stop?"

Howard poked at a piece of soggy white potato in his soup. "Your mom's had a lot of problems, Andy," he said carefully. "She might be capable of almost anything."

Andy pushed back his chair so hard it clattered onto its back. He stomped out of the room without a word, and Howard buried his face in his hands.

Changing the locks made no difference. In fact, December 4th was the worst night yet. When they got into bed, they could feel bony fingers scratching and pulling at the covers of the bed. The skin on their arms and faces tingled and itched like no-see-ums were attacking, but when Howard turned the light on, there were no bugs anywhere in the room.

Before he could even turn the lights off again, his heavy leather work shoes flew up into the air, over the bed, and smashed into the wall next to the window. Andy whimpered. The boy's houseshoes took flight, soaring over the bed as if they were hurled by a raging, invisible hand.

Andy lay in the bed, huddled beneath the covers, looking for a moment so lost and forlorn that he reminded Howard of the boy at six years old—all arms and legs and mischief. As Howard reached out for him, the boy ducked, and Howard thought his son was cringing from his own hand. But he turned to see shirts, slacks, belts, and coats materializing outside the closet door, still on their hangers, and then hurtling across the room like vacant, vicious scarecrows.

He turned out the light, helplessly listening to his son's soft moans of terror. From underneath the bed, he heard a strange, metallic scraping noise. He lay stiff, preparing for another onslaught. Something heavy jangled to the floor, then propelled itself across the room, slamming into the wall with such force that the sheetrock gave in. Howard turned on the light again and went over to examine the object. It was the handle to the gas jet beneath the bed. The gas space heater had long been disconnected, so he sighed and let the handle fall back onto the floor.

Andy began to shake uncontrollably. Howard wrapped his arms around his son and lay in the dark, wondering what else Henry Anglin had in store for them. It didn't take long to find out. With a jerk, the bed was pulled away from the wall, as if by an irate but unseen man. Howard got up, pushed the bed back against the wall, and lay down again. The bed jerked again, this time with such force that Andy nearly tumbled off the bed. He cried out, but lay as if frozen for the next fifteen minutes as his father battled against Henry Anglin, moving the bed back in place time and time again, only to have it jerked out into the center of the room.

Finally Andy broke down. "Dad," he sobbed, "you can't beat him. Don't you see that?"

Angrily Howard pulled on his pants and stuffed his wallet into his pocket. "Get dressed," he commanded the boy. "We're going to a motel."

When they went home the next morning, chaos greeted them. Scraps of paper, notes from Henry Anglin, Mrs. Snow, and Mrs. Elliot were flying everywhere, like a paper blizzard. A fat cigar whizzed through the air, narrowly missing Andy and angling suddenly upward to smack Howard sharply on the temple.

"Damn it," he exclaimed and studied it before he threw it into the trash. "Where did this come from?"

"Look, Dad!" Andy pointed, but Howard wasn't quick enough to see the cigar jump back out of the trashbasket and skitter across the floor.

Howard sat down heavily in a kitchen chair and surveyed the devastation that surrounded him. Johnnie, he decided, could not be behind all this. No matter how crazy she was, she was simply not this malevolent.

"Of course not, dummy."

Howard jumped at the voice coming from the corner above the refrigerator.

"Now, when are you going to clean this mess up?"

"I wish you could help us," he retorted. Andy picked up a can of soup off the floor and placed it on the counter. It immediately sprang up into the air and clattered onto the floor.

"I didn't do that," Mrs. Elliot said.

Behind him, on the table, Andy heard the toaster click. A nasty smell filled the kitchen, and Andy cautiously reached for the remnant of white that stuck out of the toaster's slot. It was a hotel-size bar of soap, half-melted. Floating lazily down from the ceiling was a scrap of paper. "CleAn toasTEr" it read, and the raucous laughter of Henry Anglin resounded throughout the house.

Later, Andy sat at the freshly-scrubbed kitchen table, laboriously composing a letter to his mother. Since he didn't want to tell her about events at the house, it was hard to think of things to write. But sometimes she wrote back, so he never stopped struggling.

He saw movement out of the corner of his eye and glanced at his dad, scrambling eggs at the stove. His mother's hand floated just to the right of his dad's shoulder, and something about it suggested a threat.

"Look out!" Andy shouted. Again the eerie laughter of Henry Anglin pealed through the room, and the vision of the hand disintegrated.

A week later, Andy was hunched over the secondhand guitar his dad had given him for his fourteenth birthday. He was slowly, painfully teaching himself how to pick out a few chords, and he spent hours every evening, sometimes staying up even later than his dad. A flicker of motion caused him to look up. Just outside the window was the dim outline of his mother's shape. He held his breath, not believing his eyes, and soon enough, the form dissolved into a shapeless play of shadows. A note appeared, tucking itself between the guitar strings: "MisS yOUR MoMmy?"

Andy furiously blinked back the tears that sprang into his eyes. He bit the inside of his cheek to keep from sobbing and picked so long and so fiercely at the guitar strings that his fingers began to bleed.

From that night, the number of voices Andy heard nearly doubled. There were so many people talking to him he couldn't recall all their names. Mrs. Elliot, Mrs. Snow, and Mr. Gree continued to look after him, offering solicitous advice about his choice of clothing, his appetite, and his pets.

Henry Anglin's angry voice, cruel notes and grating laughter still marked every day, for both Andy and Howard. Bugs and slugs assaulted them, if not every night, then every other night. One night, Henry Anglin woke them both from a sound sleep, demanding to be allowed to fry an egg. They ignored him, and the voice went away.

"Andy." Howard called his son to the kitchen at daybreak, a puzzled note in his voice.

"What, Dad?"

"Did you get up last night?" Howard pointed to the stove.

Andy stared in astonishment. The non-stick skillet sat on the eye of the stove—nothing remarkable since Andy often left it there to dry. But the burner was turned on low, and inside the skillet was the charred but unmistakable form of a fried egg.

"I didn't get up, Dad."

Howard swore softly. "You want a ride to school, Andy?" He left the skillet on the stove to deal with when he got home from work.

It was late spring in Tyler, Texas, 1966. U.S. bombers were preparing to bomb Hanoi, and Lyndon B. Johnson, a native of Texas, was building a Great Society, but Howard and Andy were oblivious to the larger world. Their world had shrunk to the 1,300 square feet of the house on Elizabeth Street. Getting a full night's sleep without interruption by raging voices, flying bugs, or burning food was their primary preoccupation.

"Call the police."

Howard sat upright in bed confused. Andy was asleep beside him.

"Call the cops in Houston," the voice demanded.

"No, Henry Anglin. I won't." Howard spoke loudly enough to make Andy stir beside him. Then Howard tucked his head under the covers, ready for an onslaught of bugs or slugs.

"CALL THE POLICE!" the voice roared.

"No, I won't!" Howard shouted back, stubborn.

"I won't let you go back to sleep," whispered the voice to his left.

"UNTIL YOU CALL THE POLICE!" the voice screeched in his right ear, so loud and so close Howard could almost feel the explosive breath of the "p" as it was spoken.

The voice bounced around from place to place in the room, high, low, near the window, then next to the door. "Please, please, pleeeeeaaasse!" Henry Anglin cajoled him. Andy lay awake, watching carefully for any objects that might suddenly take flight.

Andy's shoes rose up into the air, thumping against the wall to punctuate every syllable. "Call the po-lice in Hous-ton NOW! Call the po-lice in Hous-ton NOW!" The chant went on and on, alternating with long, whiny bouts of begging. The longer Henry Anglin tormented them, the more defiant Howard became.

"He's not going to do it, Mr. Anglin!" The shout bursting from Andy's mouth surprised him as much as it did his dad.

"All right, then," the voice said petulantly. "I'll let you go to sleep … if you'll take a little drive."

"Are you crazy?" Howard shouted at the wall.

Andy erupted into laughter, and after a minute, Howard joined in. There was nothing crazier than the past ten months of their life.

Andy and Howard pulled on their clothes and drove, as Henry Anglin instructed them, around the loop that circumnavigated the city of Tyler. It was three o'clock when they got in, but Henry Anglin allowed them to sleep uninterrupted until the alarm clock rang at seven.

Andy had finished the eighth grade, and at fourteen, was old enough to take care of himself in the summer while his dad went to work. During the day, he would mess around with his guitar, ride his bike, maybe go to the pool. He didn't really have any friends, unless you counted Mr. Gree, Mrs. Elliot, and Mrs. Snow. In the evenings, his dad would cook a little something, then go to his workshop to labor on a few projects. The workshop was the same confined space where Henry Anglin had first announced his presence last summer by nearly asphyxiating Howard with bug spray.

"Henry Anglin's gone," a voice said through the heating vent.

"We took care of him for you," chimed in another voice, from above the light fixture.

"What are you talking about?" Howard said sharply, setting down the tool he'd been working with.

"We took that miserable man back to his grave," explained Mrs. Elliot matter-of-factly.

"Put a stake through his heart," Mrs. Snow announced with some satisfaction.

"What are you talking about?" Howard, perplexed, dropped onto the stool he kept next to the workbench.

"Mr. Gree made it for us," Mrs. Snow said patiently.

"That should take care of it, all right," Mrs. Elliot said grandly, and Howard had a sudden memory of her replacing a broken wheel on his roller skates, years ago, dusting off her hands and pronouncing the same words, with the same definitive note of pleasure in a job well done.

"Tootle-o, dear," Mrs. Snow warbled, and Howard was left in a workshop that felt suddenly empty.

That summer and fall were relatively peaceful. Bugs flew only once or twice and never with the fury that marked the presence of Henry Anglin. In February, Johnnie came back to the house on Elizabeth Street. The three of them lived more or less like any other family in 1967, when coffee cost 59 cents a pound and a box of 'Nilla Wafers was 33 cents. On their small black-and-white TV set, they watched Tallulah Bankhead's guest appearance on *Batman* that spring and went to the drive-in movie theater to see *Dracula, Prince of Darkness*.

Mrs. Elliot, Mrs. Snow, Mr. Gree, and all the other voices were still making regular comments on the family's habits and living arrangements, but Johnnie pretended not to hear them. No one could ignore the notes that would suddenly materialize in the air and float down to the ground, though, and Howard began to receive more and more.

In the fall, Andy's interest in school dropped off dramatically. He let his hair grow as long as he dared, and the teenager started spending more and more time isolated in his room with his three cats and his guitar.

"Andy." Howard beat on the boy's door, holding a letter in his fist. "Open the door."

Andy sluggishly complied, releasing a wave of loud music as the door swung slowly in.

"I've got a letter from the school here. Turn that crap off, will you?"

When the music stopped, Howard waved the paper in Andy's face. "This says you haven't been to school in three weeks. What in God's name is going on here?"

"Mrs. Elliot said I didn't have to go to school," the boy said, sulky. "She says I should just take a correspondence course and finish high school that way."

"What a load of horse manure!" Howard slammed his fist against the wall in anger. Andy shrugged his shoulders. A note floated down from the vicinity of the hall light fixture.

"ANdy is a nervous wreCk. Let him do it mY way."

The note was signed "El."

"I'd rather go away with Mrs. Elliot than go back to school." Andy stared defiantly at his father.

"You don't even know where she is! Hell, you don't even know what she is!"

"I know she cares about me."

"Oh, my God." Howard turned away, defeated.

That night, in his workshop, Howard asked Mrs. Elliot to go away.

He felt a little funny talking to the air, but it only took a few seconds for a note to materialize in response.

"YoU caN't makE me. I'll take AnDy with me if I gO."

"Don't go, then, dammit! You're probably just a figment of my imagination anyway!" The hand holding the chisel slipped, cracking the delicate piece of wood he was working on into dozens of tiny pointed shards. He looked at the debris in his hands and saw the wreckage of his family.

In the last part of February, Henry Anglin came back. His words were audible only to Andy, but signs of his malice were everywhere. To begin with, he would steal raw eggs from the refrigerator and hide them in places that would particularly annoy Howard. He put eggs under the mattress where Howard's head was, put eggs in his shoes, a robe pocket, in the pillowcase, in the ceiling light globe. When Howard lay down and heard the crack of the egg or slipped his shoes on and realized too late what was inside, Henry's Anglin's shrieks of laughter would erupt through the house. When Henry Anglin tired of these games, he would break eggs against the wall or a chest of drawers.

March in Texas can be very pretty. The parched brown grass begins to show a little green seeping in, and the first tentative daffodils peer out from drifts of dead, dried leaves and winter's rubble. Howard was cautiously enjoying the beginning of spring one day at work when his telephone rang.

"Dad."

Howard's gut clenched up reflexively. He and Andy were barely speaking, so the call would hardly be for a casual chat about what's for dinner.

"Did you move my dresser?"

"No, of course not."

"It's on the middle of my bed. Mom says she didn't do it."

"Leave it. I'll help you move it tonight."

Howard could almost hear Andy's shrug.

"It's not that heavy. I'll get it."

The next day, a Thursday, Andy found his chest of drawers sitting right in the center of the bed. This piece was too heavy to move alone.

When Andy and Howard heaved it to the floor, grunting with the effort, they both could hear the mocking laughter of Henry Anglin.

The house was dark when Howard returned home from work on Friday. He was almost relieved. Dealing with his wife's oddities and his son's sullenness tired him more than he cared to admit. Walking down the short hall to his room, he noticed Andy's door shut. He knocked softly then grasped the handle, preparing to swing the door inwards and glance into the room.

When the door fell, angling sharply toward the floor, Howard gasped in surprise. The hinge pins had been taken out. He quickly reached his other hand to steady the door as it fell to the carpet, and then he noticed the marks.

The door, like all the other interior doors of the house, had a hollow-core construction: two flimsy pieces of veneer glued to a frame with nothing in between. An angry person—man, woman, or even child—could easily drive a fist through it. And that's exactly what had been done. Someone had struck this door repeatedly, leaving holes the size of a fist up and down the length of the veneer.

Saturday, Howard went to work to catch up on a few things. It was well past dark when the telephone rang.

"Dad." The boy sounded frightened. "He moved the whole refrigerator." Andy and Johnnie had left the house for a few hours, returning to find the refrigerator in the bedroom.

Monday night, Andy called again. The washer had been pulled loose from its plumbing fittings, leaving water spewing all over the kitchen. Howard swore, then called the police and threw on his jacket to meet them on Elizabeth Street.

The two uniformed officers were plainly unconcerned about Howard's claims of vandalism. But when they saw the interior of the house, their demeanor changed.

Johnnie sat on the sofa, smoking a cigarette. She ignored the exclamations of the men around her.

"Look at that, Frank!" The younger police officer nudged his partner, pointing to the bathroom door. It had twenty holes punched into it, in a random pattern, some fist-sized, others the size of a man's head. Every interior door had been battered, although there was no sign that a human hand had done the work. No smudges of blood marked the doors, no fragments of torn flesh hung from the jagged edges of the holes.

Before the end of February, Howard moved out of the house on Elizabeth Street. Whatever lived there had defeated him. Six weeks later, after he had found a suitable place, Andy and Johnnie joined him.

Henry Anglin, whatever he may have been in his lifetime, had become a psychic vampire. The family's hopes of building a new life, free from the stresses that had contributed to Johnnie's first illness, had all been drained away.

Whether Henry Anglin still inhabits the house on Elizabeth Street or has moved on to torment others remains a mystery. But the pain he caused is undeniable. The Beaird family's potential for happiness dwindled away, becoming as dried up and lifeless as the spirit who extracted it.

MADAME LALAURIE

 arch 19, 1862
Paris, France

My dear niece:

I must first tell you how pleased I was to receive your letter of February 3rd. I am so happy you have taken up residence in that dear city with your new husband. I know the joy of your marriage was made bittersweet by his hasty departure to join the war effort, but I remain certain that our Lord hears our prayers for his safety and will guard him until he can return to you.

How brave you are, to undertake a search for a suitable home while he is away! I was flattered by your request for advice, but I do not know how valuable my words will be for you. It has been nearly thirty years since I left the Crescent City and much has changed.

Of all the homes you mention in your letter, there is one that I would caution you against, at all costs. The mansion at 1140 Royal Street has a dark and terrible history, and I doubt anyone could ever be happy within its walls.

I can hear you now, badgering me to give you all the details. You were always the one to beg for stories, dear Kate, and I suspect that has not changed in the years since I last saw you. It is difficult for me to imagine you, a grown-up lady, with a household of her own to manage. But there—you may stop laughing at your old uncle for his wandering mind—I shall tell you the story of the house on Royal Street.

In 1832, I was a crass young thing. Yes indeed, I was young once. I had arrived in New Orleans as the fourth (and somewhat extraneous, I felt at the time) son of a plantation family. Having no other means, I had determined to make my fortune as a trader in cotton. (Now they would call me a speculator, but I was not a bit unscrupulous. Well, at least not to those who could not afford it.)

I had no small estimation of my worth in my own mind and expected to waste no time in being introduced to the better social circles. Our family was prominent in Charleston, and New Orleans was just another port city. Oh, the infinite optimism of youth!

New Orleans Society snubbed me so thoroughly it's a wonder I survived. The Creole families in that day were quite isolated from the crude, newly arrived Americans. They would no more pass the time of day with me than I would with a slave. And of course, it was their parties, their balls, their social events that drew me. So, once my wounded pride was somewhat healed, I circulated around the edges of those great families, like a poor, dowdy moth attracted to the brilliant crystal pendants of a grand chandelier.

The name on everyone's lips was Delphine Lalaurie. She was the very pinnacle of society and as far beyond me as the moon and stars. Her beauty was legendary. General LaFayette himself was honored at a dinner in her home and was struck by her charms, social and otherwise. Her husband, Louis Lalaurie, was little more than a figurehead. A source of income to finance Mme. Lalaurie's brilliant social engagements. She had been married twice before, and both husbands had died, but under what circumstances I never heard. I do not believe they were considerably older than her, however—she never struck me as the type to allow her father to marry her off to an older man, for any reason. She was well-known for her fiery temper, although her loveliness and wit allowed her to disguise it as something less than shrewishness.

Some nights, in a fit of self-pity, I would stroll down Royal Street just to see who had been honored with an invitation to the Lalaurie mansion. She had had Louis build it for her, so its parlors, dining rooms, and ballroom were all splendidly planned and opulently decorated. If I sauntered slowly enough, I could see ladies in their low-cut, elaborate gowns sweeping past the floor-length windows as they danced with men luckier than I. Sometimes a carriage would pause, and a richly attired couple alight, the coachman and butler staring with distrust at the fellow loitering on the corner with a cigar—me!

One day, I chanced to mention my desire to meet Mme. Lalaurie to a business associate of mine. He laughed.

"That woman is a hellcat," he told me. I was shocked by his strong language, and I hope you will forgive me for repeating it here. He asked if I knew all her slaves had been taken from her by the sheriff. It seems a neighbor had witnessed Mme. Lalaurie chasing a slave girl—no more than eight or ten years old—through the courtyard, beating her with a long, wicked-looking whip. Now this, as you know, is not unusual. All slaves have to be disciplined every now and then. While you and I might not agree with her methods, it is certainly within her rights.

But the appalling part of the story comes next. The neighbor heard Mme. Lalaurie chase the child all the way through the house, up to the rooftop. It is, as you have noticed, an imposing three-story structure. The child was so terrified and Mme. Lalaurie beat her so savagely, that the poor slave jumped to her death in the courtyard below.

When the sheriff investigated the neighbor's complaint, he did indeed find a mangled corpse at the bottom of a well on the Lalaurie property. Her slaves were sold at auction, supposedly to more humane owners, but Mme. Lalaurie's relatives purchased them and returned them to this queen of New Orleans Society.

It is shocking, isn't it, the disparity between a public facade and private actions? Although I was quite sobered by my friend's story, I still wanted very badly to become a part of the Lalaurie circle. Because, you see, she did not only bestow her radiance on Society. A chosen few artists, writers, gamblers, and politicians were also allowed to grace her parlors. In my arrogance, I believed she would find my wit and charm so irresistible that I would be included at her gatherings, primitive American that I was, if she only had a chance to know me.

It was this vain hope that led me to amble slowly down Dumaine Street after a late card game on the night of April 10, 1834. I was terrified to see great clouds of white smoke billowing slowly out into the street as I turned the corner onto Royal Street. The Lalaurie mansion was on fire. I joined neighbors as they rushed to the scene and stepped over the threshold to see a vibrant but calm Mme. Lalaurie pointing out her favorite pieces of furniture.

"Take this out, please," she'd say, pointing at a particularly fine mahogany side table. Teams of people leapt to do her bidding. I pulled at her sleeve, noting that a small smudge of cinders on her left cheek served only to highlight her beauty.

"Are all the people here safely out, Madame?"

I admit that I was struggling to impress her with my grace and charm even in such circumstances. I realize that you may be disappointed by my shallowness of character, but I beg you to remember that I was only a callow youth. My character is at least an inch deeper now, at the advanced age of sixty-one.

The woman looked at me and laughed. Even now, I hate to remember that sound. It had not an ounce of compassion in it. Her eyes glittered strangely, like an animal's. I drew back and all desire to become familiar with the lady died at once.

"Here, here!" Two men struggled through the thickening smoke, carrying between them a ragged, bony Negro. Heading for the door, one man threw over his shoulder a look of such loathing that I recoiled. An instant later, I realized it was not directed at me, but at the woman by my side.

The volunteer fire department arrived next, and although I did not see them at work, by some miraculous combination of modern equipment and luck, the fire was extinguished.

Outside on the pavement, the emaciated Negro was crying, and her two rescuers bent over her.

"I couldn't stand it no more! I knows it was wrong, but I rather be daid than live with that creature another minute!" It occurred to me that the woman was confessing to setting the blaze. As it turned out, she was the Lalaurie's cook, and she had been chained—yes, chained—to the kitchen floor. Mme. Lalaurie had been more concerned about her furniture than her slaves.

But worse horrors were to be revealed. The cook urged her rescuers to go to the attic, for there were more slaves there, probably restrained as she had been, or too weak to save themselves.

I went upstairs with several other men, shouldering past Mme. Lalaurie, who seemed blithely unconcerned. What we saw in that attic is too gruesome to describe. That woman had systematically tortured, with the most hellishly contrived instruments, untold numbers of slaves. She had not stopped at torture, either. We found evidence of activities which no Christian, no rational human being, would engage in. We rescued those slaves still alive, but for some, we arrived too late.

A crowd had gathered outside, attracted by the excitement of the fire. They stayed to see the shocking condition of the creatures who had come under Mme. Lalaurie's power. These slaves had been so mistreated, so cruelly used, that the good people of New Orleans cried out to have Mme. Lalaurie punished for her crimes. But, alas, membership in Society often gives advantages to those least deserving, and such was the case that spring night. We waited, and waited, and waited for the sheriff to arrive.

Mme. Lalaurie laughed and chatted with her friends, strolling through the house, replacing items of furniture that had been carried out from the fire. We could see her through the brightly lit windows. Finally, it became more than the crowd could bear. It became a mob and pushed and shoved and roared, trying to find a way into the Lalaurie mansion. To avoid being trampled, I climbed up a lamppost. From that vantage point I could see a fine carriage thundering down Royal Street, driven by the very butler who had eyed me suspiciously as I lingered around the Lalaurie mansion.

"Here she comes!" I shouted and leapt down to grab the reins and pull those galloping horses to a stop.

The sound of hooves bearing down on you must be one of the most terrifying sounds on earth. But my rage, and, curiously, my sense of betrayal, was equal to the great respect which I had awarded Mme. Lalaurie before this night. I felt she had to be stopped, at any cost.

My hands reached for and grabbed the leather bridle. I felt the fittings slither through my fingers and looked up in triumph, just in time to see the lashes of a great bull whip. Some instinct led me to throw up my hands and cover my face. That saved my eyes from the stinging agony of the whip, but as you know, I carry a scar on my hand to this day, a memento of Mme. Lalaurie.

Somehow, she managed to escape. It was said that she went to Europe with Dr. Lalaurie.

You asked me why I left New Orleans. I think it has to do with a weakness, a defect, in my character. New Orleans is a lush, rich, tropical city. I remember being amazed, in December, at how much greenery surrounded me. But that atmosphere of fertile growth, of possibilities, is not for the fainthearted. I believe such warm, humid vapors have the power to corrupt the soul, just as they corrupt other materials. I felt myself, after only a few months, consumed by a lassitude of spirit that threatened to end my dreams. I had to leave. But I still have not, after all my wanderings, found my home.

Perhaps that same atmosphere can have a different effect on different people. For Mme. Lalaurie, born and bred there, it may have turned her into a monster. Some people have circulated strange tales about her activities. Perhaps, it is said, she had a curious desire, or even need, to hurt people. To see their blood. Perhaps, even, to taste it.

But I do not intend to populate your dreams with horror, dear girl. If Mme. Lalaurie was a vampire or a ghoul or just an evil woman, she is gone now. And there is an interesting story surrounding her death.

I do not know if you have ever been boar-hunting, but believe me when I tell you it is the most savage of sports. A thousand-pound creature, with eyes glowing red as the devil's, hurls itself at you with all its might. During the course of the hunt, it is tortured, stabbed, and purposely abused, to make better sport. Mme. Lalaurie enjoyed this type of diversion, and remembering the torment of her slaves, I can see why. Anyway, she was boar-hunting in the South of France one fine day and

MADAME LALAURIE

her gun jammed. God's justice, perhaps. She tried to beat the ferocious creature back with her whip (the same one, I wonder?), but failed. The boar fell upon her, piercing her chest with his tusks. She was staked through the heart, which, as everyone knows, is the best way to kill a vampire.

Well I have gone on too long, dear niece, and probably told you far more than you wished to hear. But I do hope you will avoid that house on Royal Street, in spite of its excellent price. Even if Mme. Lalaurie no longer inhabits it, in any form, surely the anguish of her victims lives on. I would far prefer to think of you in some neat little cottage, with children tumbling about in the yard, than to envision you in that sterile mansion filled with past horrors.

Please do write again, soon.

Your obedient servant,

Uncle Philip

THE ACE OF HEARTS

he click, click of a cane tapping on the flagstone sidewalk came precisely at eight o'clock, sending the ladies within the fine old mock Tudor home into a frenzy of twittering.

"Oh, do set that bowl of nuts down here, Martha," exclaimed one lady, her thin fingers nervously touching her hair, just blued and set that day by Arthur, in the village.

"I never did like this dress! Why did I wear this one?" another lady queried of herself, as she examined her reflection in a mirror.

Martha set the bowl of nuts down with a slight thump and demanded, "Well, is anyone going to get the door?" although their guest had not yet touched the ornate brass door knocker.

All three ladies headed for the door, at varying speeds, depending on their physical condition and their perception of their own dignity. Martha, the youngest and most agile and the least likely to take herself seriously, reached the door first.

Phyllis, her senior by a scant two years, murmured to herself, "Well, I do think she could let me get the door at my own house!" Her tone was laced with acid yet dripping with that peculiar kind of cloying sweetness inbred in a certain class of Southern women.

Agatha, having left the mirror to attend the door, wondered if her lipstick had smeared onto her dentures—a most unappetizing sight, she worried.

"Mr. D'Aggacy!" cried Martha, flinging the door open wide. "How wonderful!"

"Welcome to my house, Mr. D'Aggacy," said Phyllis, rather formally.

"How good to *see* you, dear," said Agatha, presuming on her earlier friendship—she had been the first to meet this charming man six months ago, at the community center's annual open house.

"What a splendid house!" Mr. D'Aggacy exclaimed. "Its beauty is eclipsed only by the loveliness of its inhabitants."

Each woman responded to this flattery according to her character: Martha, good natured and immensely practical, relished it as the compliment it was intended. Phyllis, accustomed to royal treatment after years at the top of the city's best society, accepted it as her due. And poor Agatha, whose dear John had abandoned her after years of domestic bliss (though not by choice—by angina), was still too attuned to her apparent shortcomings to believe a word of it.

"Well, shall we begin?" asked Phyllis, gesturing dramatically towards the game table set up in the parlor. As the foursome moved through the foyer to the parlor, Agatha glanced again at the mirror. Something was odd about the picture the group presented there. One, two, three figures, Agatha counted, almost unconsciously. But the moment quickly passed, and she dismissed the thought as they seated themselves, their expressions becoming serious. Bridge was more than a passion—it was their connection to life, and maintaining that connection a time-consuming occupation. They cut the cards to see who would partner whom.

"One heart," Phyllis opened.

With a look of intense concentration, Agatha arranged and rearranged the cards in her hand. She shot a look at Mr. D'Aggacy, her partner, across the table, who nodded and smiled reassuringly.

"Pass."

"Pass," said Martha.

"Pass," Mr. D'Aggacy said.

Agatha led with a ten of clubs, and play began in earnest.

When the party was breaking up, near eleven, Phyllis's phone rang shrilly. With a look of consternation—after a certain age, late phone calls never brought good news—Phyllis disappeared into the back hallway to answer it. When she returned, her face was a bit pale.

"That was my niece," she told her friends. "Her mother-in-law has had a stroke, and she's in the hospital."

"Oh, my," said Agatha. "Here, honey, sit down," and she guided the shaken woman to a brocade settee next to the fireplace.

"I'll get you a little sherry, dear, to settle you," said Martha. She went to the sideboard in the dining room and poured a healthy slug of wine from the crystal decanter into a waiting glass. Mr. D'Aggacy remained by Phyllis's side, holding her hand as he perched on the sofa beside her.

"Had she been ill before?" he inquired solicitously.

"Why, no, she was always disgustingly athletic. She had those little muscles in her arms, you know, because she insisted on carrying her own bag when she played golf. Really, this is quite a shock."

"I'll go with you to see her tomorrow, Phyllis, before our three o'clock game," offered Agatha. "I knew her from the club, and didn't she take ceramics or something at the community center?"

"Yes, yes, something like that," Phyllis said vaguely. Having bolted the sherry, she was beginning to feel its fortifying effects. "I'll call you and pick you up about one-thirty."

"Do you need anything else, Phyllis?" said Martha as she gathered her purse and sweater.

"I'm fine, dear, thank you," said Phyllis, still seated. "Only don't mind me not showing you out. I'm still. . . do you know she came out at the Camellia Ball just three years before me."

"Well, but you're so much more sensible, dear," reassured Agatha. "I'm sure all that *strenuous* activity wasn't good for her."

After wishing Mr. D'Aggacy a pleasant evening, Martha and Agatha made their way to the foyer, shutting the door gently behind them.

"I am so sorry this has upset you so," Mr. D'Aggacy said softly, still patting her hand gently. "It is disturbing when someone close to you is taken ill."

"Catherine's husband worked in the same firm as my dear Horace did, you know, so she and I often spent time together. But we weren't really close," said Phyllis.

"A stroke is a terrible kind of illness," mused Mr. D'Aggacy.

Phyllis started, nearly jerking her hand out of his with her abrupt movement. "Why, that's just what I was thinking, Mr. D'Aggacy!"

"My father had a stroke," he continued, "and his suffering — and my mother's—just dragged on and on."

"Oh, yes," breathed Phyllis. "My grandmother had a stroke and lived with us for five long years before she passed away. My poor mother had to live with that every day—she drooled, you know, and, um, couldn't care for herself."

"Yes, it's so sad, to see their bright eyes and know that they're in there, just unable to help themselves or speak. My father would get angry sometimes and make the most agonizing noises," Mr. D'Aggacy confided.

"This is just amazing, Mr. D'Aggacy," Phyllis said, her eyes wide. "My grandmother did that exact same thing. I used to have nightmares about it."

"To lose control of one's destiny is the most frightening thing we all face," mused the handsome old gentleman. "I hope I would be spared that indignity."

"Oh, yes," said Phyllis fervently. "I hope when my time comes it's fast. Catherine's husband died of cancer, you know, and lingered on, in a great deal of pain. I do hope she recovers quickly."

Mr. D'Aggacy gave her hand a final pat as he rose to his feet. "Well, I must be going, dear Phyllis," he said. "I have enjoyed our little chat so much."

"Forgive me for being nosy, Mr. D'Aggacy," Phyllis said as they walked toward the foyer. "But where is your family from? Your name, it sounds French, but you don't have a bit of an accent."

"Well, we're from all over, actually," Mr. D'Aggacy replied with a slight smile. "My mother's family was from Eastern Europe, and my father's family had estates in France."

"Oh, I see," said Phyllis, although his answer hadn't really satisfied her curiosity. "Don't forget your lovely walking stick." She handed it to him, then glanced closer at the pattern cut into the dark, polished mahogany. "Are those birds?" The creatures covering the surface had strange ribbed wings outstretched, and she thought she saw pointed ears before he swung the stick out over the threshold.

"Have a pleasant evening, Phyllis," he called as he went down the walk. "Thank you for your hospitality. I now understand why Southerners are famous for it!"

What a gallant man, Phyllis thought as she went through the ritual of switching off porch lights, turning on security lights, setting the alarm system, and throwing the deadbolt home to its socket. How mysterious—and what a pleasant change from the mundane companions of her ordinary life.

The next day, Martha was just pulling up to the community center when Phyllis and Agatha arrived. "How is Catherine today?" she inquired as the three ladies walked toward the door of the low, white clapboard house where they had all met.

"I'm afraid it was a very severe stroke," sighed Agatha, holding Phyllis's arm protectively. "She will probably never recover enough to go home."

"They'll send her to a nursing home," stated Phyllis flatly. "And knowing Anthony, she'll be abandoned there."

"What about your niece, Phyllis? Stacy, is that her name?" Martha held the door open for all three.

"Stacy is much too busy to concern herself with Catherine," snorted Phyllis. "Catherine never had much use for Stacy anyway. What goes around, comes around."

The ladies were silent for a moment, unable to resist comparing their situations with that of the stricken Catherine. At least, Martha thought, my Thomas would try to take care of me at home. I've always gotten along well with his wife. But would I want to live with them? She didn't share her thoughts with Phyllis, who had nowhere to go. Poor Phyllis, she thought.

"Well," Martha said brightly, laying down her purse. "Who's making up a foursome today?"

"It'll probably be that Mrs. Webb character," grumbled Phyllis. "She always giggles when she bids."

"I do wish Mr. D'Aggacy would join us," exclaimed Agatha. "What *does* he do all day, anyway?"

"We should schedule more evening games," said Martha. "He's such a delightful partner. And so polite, even when things aren't going his way."

"He rarely loses," pointed out Phyllis. "It's almost as if he knows what cards will be played before they're on the table."

Once Agatha got a question in her mind, she worried at it like a terrier. "Really, why won't he play in the daytime? He is retired, isn't he, and he doesn't have any family here, does he?"

"You are full of questions, today, Agatha!" Martha poked gentle fun at her friend as she began to shuffle the cards. "Curiosity killed the cat, you know!"

"Mr. D'Aggacy is a very private man," Phyllis stated.

The fourth player arrived, and the women lost themselves in their game, as usual.

On Thursday evening the little community center overlooking the park was brightly lit. Enough players arrived to set up several tables, but Phyllis, Martha and Agatha held themselves apart, awaiting the arrival of the chivalrous Mr. D'Aggacy.

"Ah, there you are, dear," cried Phyllis, heading for the tall, slender figure impeccably attired in a suit just slightly out of style. She bore down on him like an ocean liner, stately, serene, and unstoppable. "We've saved a special table for the four of us."

Mr. D'Aggacy politely inquired after the health of the three widows as they settled themselves down for an evening of play. Although they did not chat during the course of the game—it was much too important an endeavor to waste time in idle chatter—during a short break, Mr. D'Aggacy turned to Phyllis.

"How is your dear friend Catherine?" he asked with genuine concern.

"Oh, she was sent off to a nursing home today. Some hole named Fair Haven or Rose Manor or something like that." Phyllis fiddled with her pearls, an unusual sign of agitation in a lady of her breeding. "I imagine she'll live there for the next ten or fifteen years, wearing a bib and stuffed into a wheelchair on Sundays."

Mr. D'Aggacy touched her elbow lightly but did not respond. Just then another regular bridge player arrived at their table holding a tray of canapés.

"Anyone ready for hors d'oeuvres?" she bubbled. "The cooking class made these today, and they are absolutely delish!"

Martha studied them suspiciously. "What's in them?" she asked. The little round crackers were covered with a thin layer of a pink paste, and garnished with a bit of green—maybe parsley, she thought.

"Oh, I'm feeling adventurous tonight," declared Agatha, and she popped a cracker into her mouth. "It's good," she pronounced. "Y'all try one."

Mr. D'Aggacy delicately nibbled on one edge of a cracker, then set it down, saying it didn't agree with him.

Agatha had several more, while Martha and Phyllis declined, preferring their Diet Cokes. "Mr. D'Aggacy, you look a little green," said Martha abruptly. "Are you feeling all right?"

"Yes, yes," he said quickly. "I've just had a busy day, but thank you for your concern." They began to play again, quietly except for brisk rounds of bidding and occasional exclamations of pleasure or dismay.

"Mercy, Agatha, stop breathing on me," complained Martha. "Your breath could kill a dragon."

"I'm sorry, Martha." Agatha's hand flew to cover her mouth, mortified. "Those canap≥s were loaded with garlic. I should have known better."

Bridge night ended around ten o'clock, and all the players returned to their cars, commenting on the balmy night lit by the benevolent face of the full moon. "I think I'll go visit poor Catherine tomorrow, Agatha," Phyllis said as she unlocked the door of her Lincoln. "Would you care to come along?"

"Oh, yes, dear, I'd be glad to," Agatha stopped to mentally review her schedule for Friday. "I've got an appointment at Arthur's at ten and luncheon with my daughter-in-law at one. Could I meet you somewhere after that?"

"Yes, let's just meet there. It's Fair View, on Crescent Avenue. Two-thirty?"

"See you then, dear!" Agatha waved, and slammed her door shut. Phyllis noticed her dress hanging out the car door and waved to stop her friend, but Agatha just smiled gaily and nodded, oblivious.

Other car doors slammed too, and Phyllis sank into the plush seat to prepare for the short cruise down Main Street to Grove Street and the big house she lived in all alone. As she pulled out of the parking lot, a tall figure emerged from the shadows cast by massive old oak trees in the park. "Crescent Avenue," he muttered, patting down his pockets. "Now, where did I put that pen?"

On Friday afternoon, Agatha smiled her way through another deadly dull luncheon with her daughter-in-law. When will that girl understand, she thought, that I simply don't care how many diapers her child prodigy goes through in a day? Agatha loved her grandson, but didn't understand her daughter-in-law's obsessive preoccupation with "parenting." Taking nouns and making them into verbs is positively ridiculous, she thought. Ah, Crescent Avenue.

Phyllis's long dark-blue car was already parked out front, so Agatha snatched the pot of mums she'd brought out of the trunk and trotted up to the door.

"You won't need those," Phyllis announced, meeting her at the entrance. "Catherine passed away peacefully in her sleep last night."

Agatha's mouth dropped open. "But she was fine on Sunday!" she wailed.

"If you consider not being able to walk, talk, or use the bathroom by yourself fine, I guess she was!" snapped Phyllis. She steered Agatha outside.

"I don't understand," said Agatha.

"Well, the doctors are a bit surprised," Phyllis admitted. "But I'm glad she won't have to just waste away here, ignored by all the people she cared for all these years."

"You didn't really like her that much, did you?" Agatha dropped her voice to a conspiratorial whisper.

"That's beside the point," Phyllis hissed. "I was Brought Up Right, and I Know My Duty. You're supposed to take care of people who are ill whether you like them or not. Whether it's convenient or not!" She glared at Agatha with such fury that Agatha wilted.

"When's the service?" she asked when she recovered.

"They don't know yet. The doctors want an autopsy."

Inside Fair View, Catherine's relatives were also furious. "I don't know why you don't just leave her in peace!"

"It's just a little unusual, because her heart was very strong," one of the doctors tried to placate Catherine's son. "It only means a day's delay."

"Well, I can't stand around all day. I've got to get back to my office!" The middle-aged man stormed out.

The doctor sighed. "Will you sign the release, please, Mrs. Williams?" she asked. Without a word, the well-groomed woman signed the form, angling her fingers with great dexterity so her curved, two-inch talons didn't interfere with the pen. She stalked out, and the doctor turned to Fair View's administrator, shaking her head.

"What do you make of those puncture wounds, Bob?"

Death was a fairly common occurrence at Fair View. But the two small holes just below Catherine Williams's left ear were a disturbing deviation from the norm. The administrator wouldn't comment, just shook his head before offering the doctor a cup of coffee.

On Saturdays the three bridge cronies liked to gather for a cup of coffee and a pastry at a small cafe in their neighborhood. Around nine-thirty, they'd gather their purses and packages and stroll down the block to the community center for their fifth—and last—series of games for the week.

This Saturday, Martha was already established at a corner booth when Phyllis came in. Agatha would, as usual, fly in about nine-fifteen, flustered, with some tale about misplaced keys or lost kittens or recalcitrant car engines.

"Sorry about Catherine, Phyllis," Martha said. She'd talked to Agatha, so she kept her condolences short until she knew how they would be received.

"I'm not," said Phyllis shortly. "Coffee, please, and do make sure the cream is fresh," she commanded the waitress.

"There's been a rash of deaths in nursing homes lately," commented Martha, tapping her church newsletter. "Four of our parishioners died in the last two months, all of them unexpectedly, in nursing homes."

"People do die," Phyllis said. She sniffed at the pitcher of cream. Last week, the cream had curdled when it struck her coffee, and that had put her off coffee for four days. "Especially when they're old and put away. That's what they're supposed to do in nursing homes—die."

"Well, Carol May Jackson had just been diagnosed with cancer of the liver. She was going to die, but it would have taken her several months and a lot of pain. But she went to sleep one night and never woke up."

"She took cooking classes at the community center, didn't she." Phyllis wasn't really paying attention, she was trying to flag down the waitress who was contending with a rowdy table of seven fraternity boys who had just sat down.

"You probably don't remember Anna Lou Westhaven," continued Martha after a sip of coffee. "She used to paint the most awful still lifes. Her bananas looked like they were being consumed from within by some kind of fungus."

"This cream just won't do," Phyllis informed the waitress, who had finally navigated past the fraternity boys to their booth. The harried young woman took the cream pitcher and left.

"She had a series of small strokes," Martha said.

"Who? That waitress?" asked Phyllis, startled.

"No, dear, Anna Lou," Martha said patiently. "Nothing's wrong with that cream. I've been putting it in my coffee all morning."

"Well it looked funny to me." Phyllis crossed her arms across her bosom, and Martha knew the subject was closed.

"The other two, I didn't know them very well, and they were supposed to die anyway. Still, it's odd."

"Nothing's odd about dying. Let's talk about something else." The conversation turned to roses, another passion of Phyllis's and a subject in which Martha occasionally dabbled.

On Monday, Martha called Agatha and arranged to meet her before the three-o'clock bridge game.

"You know, next Tuesday's Phyllis's birthday," Martha said. "I want to have a party for her and invite everyone."

"She won't like everyone knowing it's her birthday," warned Agatha. "Last year, she wouldn't speak to me for a week just because I sent her a card."

"Pooh," said Martha. "Birthdays are for celebrating. Should we have it before or after bridge?"

"Bridge on Tuesdays starts at seven-thirty. Shouldn't we have it before?"

"I suppose. I'll call half our group, and you call the other half. Here's a list."

Agatha scanned the list. "You're calling Mr. D'Aggacy?"

"Yesssss," purred Martha. "Such a charming man."

Agatha said nothing, only blushed. If her dear John knew what she was thinking, he would probably blow a fuse. Perhaps it was just as well. . . no, that was a very uncivil thought.

"Maybe the baker at Piggly Wiggly could decorate a cake with a suit of cards," she suggested.

"That's a wonderful idea." Martha made a note, then closed up her pad and pen in her purse with a snap. "Come on, and don't tell Phyllis. I'll ask her to come over and check out the black spot on my Lizzie Horstman next Tuesday."

Martha hurried home right after bridge to begin calling birthday party guests. She called Mr. D'Aggacy first, remembering with curiosity his nocturnal habits. To her surprise, he did not answer his phone. So where, she wondered, could he be? If he wouldn't go to bridge except at night, and she knew he didn't have a job, and he didn't have any family, then why wouldn't he be at home? The question gnawed at her all afternoon and early evening as she called the other people on her list. Just at dusk, she finished calling and returned to his name and number at the top of her list.

The telephone's ring hummed in her ear as she puttered around the kitchen, thinking about what to prepare for supper. Just as she was about to hang up—the cord wouldn't quite let her reach the freezer where she had a tasty bit of beef waiting for her meal—Mr. D'Aggacy's smooth voice answered.

"Why, hello," Martha stammered. "I didn't expect. . . that is, I was about to hang up."

"Martha, what a pleasant surprise!" he cried, as if he'd been waiting all day for her call.

"I was wondering, that is, I was calling," Martha was amazed at her fast slide into adolescent awkwardness. "Phyllis's birthday —you know Phyllis. . ."

"Yes, indeed, a charming lady. Quite delightful."

"Well Agatha and I are planning a little get-together before bridge next Tuesday, and I do hope you can make it. It would mean so much to Phyllis, I know." Now I'm gushing, thought Martha. Oh, this is truly embarrassing.

"At what time would this be, my dear?"

"Well, we were thinking, that is, bridge starts at seven-thirty, so we thought about six, if that doesn't interfere with supper."

Mr. D'Aggacy laughed. "Not at all, I'm accustomed to dining late, the European custom, you know."

Martha answered his laugh with a sound that was absurdly close to a giggle. "That's wonderful, and you know, we're playing Wednesday morning at ten, Mr. D'Aggacy. If you can make it we sure would enjoy your company."

"Oh, I'm afraid I would just be wasting your time," he replied. "My skills need sharpening before I confront you ladies. I'm at my best in the evenings."

"I've never heard you mention your work before, Mr. D'Aggacy," Martha pressed on, heedless. "Have you been retired long?"

"It's been ages since I had a regular job, dear, but I really must run. I'm looking forward to tomorrow evening and the little gathering next week. Thank you so much for including me."

He is slippery, Martha thought as he hung up the phone. We haven't got a clue as to who his family is or where he's from or even where he lives now. And yet every lady who comes in contact with him is utterly charmed. And instead of being suspicious—Agatha says I'm the biggest cynic she's ever met—I'm sort of excited by this mystery.

She picked up the phone again and called her son. He worked for the telephone company. "Thomas," she barked into his voice mail (she never could speak normally to the blasted machines), "I need the address of a man, his name is D'Aggacy, D as in dog, apostrophe, A, double G, A, C, Y, and his telephone number is 833 - 0908."

It was only after she hung up that it occurred to her how her son might feel about his 60-some-odd-year-old mother using his connections to track down a man. The thought made her laugh, a belly laugh this time, not some simpering giggle.

Thomas called her back the next afternoon, just as Martha was preparing her grocery list.

"Mother, you know I'm not supposed to give out information on customers," he said without preamble.

"Yes, dear, and I always told you that three cookies was the limit, but you never had less than five. Have you suddenly grown an affinity for keeping rules?"

His mother was like a wall of water, he thought. There's no use in even trying to get around her. "Let's say I just happened to let it slip that a certain customer at 804 79th Place South never makes calls before eight at night. That's curious. Tell him he could save some money with our measured-service plan. On second thought, don't. Who is this character, anyway?"

"Never mind, dear. Are you and Sharon and the boys coming over Sunday after church?"

"Why don't you come to our house, Mom? Sharon can cook and save you the trouble."

"I like to cook." Her tone was flat, which Thomas would take as a warning if he were slightly more perceptive.

"I worry about you living all alone."

"Let's not start that, Thomas. When I start leaving the gas on, or people see me at the grocery store wearing house slippers instead of shoes, then you can talk to me about a change. But I'm not old and senile just yet. Kiss the boys for me." She hung up, slightly irritated. She looked at the grocery list and added "pot roast"—Thomas's favorite Sunday dinner. She would show him that she was in full possession of her faculties!

Then Martha laughed. What would she do, hit him over the head with the roast? Thomas was, she thought wryly, a doubter by nature. Something she could never have known when she named him forty-two years ago. Did he grow to suit the name or had some mysterious force propelled her to tag him with the name of the most skeptical disciple?

At the grocery store, she started to wad up the list and toss it in the garbage can on her way out the door. But at the bottom, she noticed the scribbled address for Mr. D'Aggacy. She absentmindedly tipped the sack boy a quarter after he loaded the bags into the trunk, oblivious to his look of scorn as he held the quarter in the flat of his palm. Martha had been tipping sack boys a quarter since she was twenty-two and newly married. Then it had been just a bit extravagant.

She checked her wristwatch and tried to ignore the plan formulating in the back of her mind. She knew spying was about as low as a lady could go. In fact, Thomas would think it was a bit crazy. Senile, even. But yet. . .

Almost against her conscious will she turned right out of the grocery store parking lot, instead of left, toward the gracious old homes and imposing trees of her neighborhood. As she headed east and then north, a delicious sense of rebellion welled up inside her, beginning in her stomach and flowing quickly to her head, like champagne. She would only drive by, just to see where he lived, she told herself. Really, what could be more harmless?

As she pulled off the main road into a residential area, she was surprised by the neighborhood where Mr. D'Aggacy lived. It was distinctly middle class, maybe even working class, with little bungalows jostling up against each other, and cheaply constructed apartment complexes placed like random scars here and there. Its only redeeming feature, she thought from her perspective of a life lived almost exclusively over-the-mountain, were the trees. Planted when the bungalows were new, they now towered over the streets, guarding them with gnarled, outstretched arms.

She turned onto Mr. D'Aggacy's street, the excitement of her illicit excursion threatening to bubble over. There were very few cars in the driveways; most families here were two-income households, and everyone was at work. What few cars there were had weeds growing out of the cracks around the tires, indicating that their capacity for movement had long been curtailed.

Martha slowed as she passed the house, a neat little white shingled dwelling, with sprightly blue shutters adorning the front windows. The shades were all tightly drawn, and there was no car out front.

She circled the block, feeling oddly unfulfilled. Seeing his house told her nothing about the man who had so captivated the ladies at the community center. But, she thought sternly, admonishing herself, any further exploration would surely be not just immoral but illegal.

Approaching 79th Place again, she threw her car into park at the corner of the cross street. "What on earth am I doing?" she thought, horrified yet strangely thrilled at her daring. She climbed out of the car, clutching her handbag and checking twice to make sure she had her keys before slamming the car door shut and locked. This looked like a dangerous part of town.

Martha giggled at the thought. Here she was, about to trespass on an innocent man's property, worried about thieves! She tried to walk normally, around the corner and down the sidewalk, pretending she was just another Jehovah's Witness. But they come in pairs, don't they? she thought giddily, now walking purposefully up the sidewalk of the little white house. She knocked loudly at the door, somehow certain there would be no answer and completely unprepared if Mr. D'Aggacy should answer.

There was no response, and she stood on tiptoe to peer through the little window at the top of the door. She was disappointed at the view. All she could see were white walls and the edge of a door frame to the left, presumably leading to the hallway, kitchen, and bedrooms. There were no decorations on the wall she could see, and she got the unexpected feeling that the house was not occupied.

Martha still felt unsatisfied. She still had no clue as to the character of this intriguing man, other than the fact that he seemed to have less money than the people she normally associated with. She stood on the porch and surveyed the quiet street beyond. No cars had passed during the minutes she had been there, and the only sound was the distant barking of a dog, several blocks over.

Again Martha moved without any conscious decision down the stairs and to the left of the house, where the bedrooms of the house were located. As if in a trance, she stretched to the top of her toes, clutching the windowsill with one hand, her purse with the other. She still couldn't see anything. The shades were drawn tightly, flush to the windowsill inside.

The bathroom window was next, she guessed, because it was higher and smaller than the two windows flanking it. Too high for her to see. But the air-conditioning unit stood below the window, mutely inviting her to step up and take a look inside. Amazed at herself, she set her purse beside it and clambered up onto the metal box. It creaked but did not sag, and she saw the shade was pulled a little crooked, offering a scant two-inch portal for her questing gaze.

As her eyes adjusted to the gloom within, she could just make out an old sink attached to the wall on the left and next to that, a toilet. There was no shower curtain surrounding the bathtub, and the old-fashioned ceramic towel racks were empty. The only sign of life was a small glass on the edge of the sink, and she smiled to see the shadowy shape of dentures within the liquid. As she stared, the dentures' shape became more clearly delineated, and it took a moment for her to comprehend why their shape struck a jarring note.

Instead of the normal, rather dainty points of the front incisors, both top and bottom were elongated, spear-shaped, sharp, and wicked looking.

Just then, a hand touched her gently on the arm. She screeched, jumped and turned at the same moment, nearly loosing her balance.

"Steady, there," said a burly black man wearing a blue-and-white striped shirt. "Can I help you?" He held her arm as she stepped down off the air-conditioning unit.

She covered her face with hands that shook wildly. "Oh, my." She cast about in her mind for a plausible story. The shock of discovery was relieved somewhat by the fact that a stranger—she squinted and stared at his shirt—apparently a meter reader for the power company —had found her. Her brain began to function again, and she smoothly spun her story.

"My, uh, nephew lives here," she said. "He hasn't been to see me in three or four days, and I was worried about him." She stepped away from the man, gathering her dignity like the folds of a cloak.

He stared at her, taking in the sight of a very well-dressed lady, with a substantial leather handbag and carefully arranged white hair. He'd seen a lot of strange things in his career, and this apparent Peeping Tom was not the strangest.

"Would you like me to call the police for you?" he asked politely, sure of her answer.

"No, no, that's quite all right," she said, dismissive, smoothing the skirt of her dress down with her hands. "I shall call his mother." Martha turned and crossed the yard, moving almost regally toward her car on the corner. The meter reader shook his head and went back to work.

At bridge that evening, Martha joined another threesome to play, avoiding Phyllis and Agatha. Soon after seven-thirty, Mr. D'Aggacy arrived, and Martha flushed when he crossed the room to speak to her. She played poorly and was glad when the evening was over. Agatha hurried over to her car in the parking lot.

"What's wrong, dear?" Agatha inquired anxiously. "You look like you've seen a ghost!"

If she only knew, thought Martha grimly. "I'll be all right, Agatha," she said shortly. "You be careful, now."

Martha couldn't sleep that night, in spite of the milk she warmed up at eleven and the little jolt of sherry she poured at one. At two, she gave it up and sat at her kitchen table, drawing up a list of names.

"Twelve women," she mused, when her list was complete. "All affiliated with the community center. All had strokes or were diagnosed with a terminal illness. And they all died in nursing homes."

She recalled Phyllis's assertion that people naturally die in nursing homes. And then she pulled out her church directory and her community center newsletters and began to make notes by each name.

It took nearly two hours, but when she was done, a clear pattern began to emerge. Each of the women had lived alone. They were widowed or had never married. Their children, if they had any, seemed unconcerned. In short, these were women whose futures as invalids were dubious at best.

But still, thought Martha. Still, to bring their lives to an end. . .she didn't want to finish that thought. She was worried about her friends and appalled that they could have so easily accepted an evil creature in their circle.

Around dawn, Martha began to remember the deep horror Phyllis had felt when her niece's mother-in-law had a stroke. She remembered the stories she'd heard of older people, unloved and forgotten, shoved into a corner of a nursing home and out of mind for relatives too busy to care. She remembered her gratitude for having a family, as irritating as they might be sometimes, who would without question take her in and care for her. And her heart softened a little bit toward Mr. D'Aggacy.

When the sun was fully up and Martha was scrambling egg substitute for breakfast, she swept her scraps of paper, lists, and doodles off the table and into the trash. Surely, this all had to be coincidence. Surely, there was no evil thing prowling around, preying on helpless old ladies. Why, Thomas would surely put her away for even thinking such things!

Martha's doorbell rang at nine, just as she was dressing for the ten-o'clock bridge game. Agatha stood there, so forlorn and lost looking that Martha's heart skipped a beat.

"Whatever happened?" she cried, leading Agatha into the living room.

Agatha's eyes filled with tears, and she sobbed against Martha's shoulder when Martha pulled her close. "It's Phyllis," she choked. "She's in the hospital."

"Why? What happened?" Martha demanded again.

"Her neighbor found her in the yard last night, next to her roses," Agatha said, straightening up and fumbling for a handkerchief. "That's all I know, I just went to pick her up for bridge, and the neighbor saw me."

"Let me get my bag, and we'll go," Martha said, standing up. "What hospital?"

"University, the neighbor said," Agatha replied. "Martha, hadn't you better put on some shoes?"

Martha looked down and saw she had on her feet her worn, scuffed house slippers. "Don't tell Thomas," she warned, kicking them off and darting down the hall to get a pair of loafers. Agatha just stood in the living room, bewildered.

"I'm afraid it's a stroke," the nurse explained gently to the two women as they stood at the foot of Phyllis's bed. "Her niece said there was a family history of stroke?"

Agatha was too distraught to answer. Martha nodded and asked what would happen next.

"Well, as soon as she's medically stable, which should be soon, we'll move her to a nursing home. There is no immediate family to take her in?"

"No," Martha sadly shook her head.

The nurse said kindly, "There's an opening at Rose Manor. I have an aunt there. They'll take good care of her."

Agatha whispered urgently to Martha in the corner of the hospital room.

Martha took Agatha by the shoulders and shook her gently. "No, Agatha, that's crazy!" she said. "Neither one of us is physically strong enough to care for her, and she'd just be miserable!"

Agatha sobbed again. "But she just hates nursing homes," she protested.

"Look, Agatha, she doesn't even know what's going on," Martha said, knowing she lied even as she spoke the words. "It won't make any difference."

Martha again spent a nearly sleepless night. Toward dawn, she climbed into her car and drove several miles east, then north into a neighborhood socially so far distant from her own that it might as well have been on the moon. On the doorstep of a modest little cottage, she left a cryptic note.

"Tomorrow. Rose Manor. Phyllis needs you."

The viewing was held at night, at the city's most prestigious funeral home. The open coffin was surrounded by what seemed to be acres and acres of flowers, many of them the dainty old-fashioned roses that Phyllis had so loved. Streams of people flowed in and out all evening, acquaintances from Phyllis's church and country club, her husband's firm, her old school friends, her garden club associates. Martha and Agatha acted as hostesses since Phyllis's niece Stacy had been unable to stay for longer than a few minutes.

Just at nine, when the viewing was scheduled to be over, Martha felt a presence at her elbow. She turned to see the dapper Mr. D'Aggacy, neatly attired as always, with an appropriately sad look on his face.

"Oh, Mr. D'Aggacy, I'm so glad you could come," Agatha said. "Phyllis enjoyed your company so much."

He bowed slightly over Agatha's hand and murmured words of sympathy.

"Well, you know, I can't help but feel that this was for the best," Agatha confided. "You know, her grandmother had a stroke and lived on for years. That made such an impression on Phyllis, and she hated the thought of being dependent on others for her care."

Mr. D'Aggacy studied Phyllis's face, framed by the satin lining of the coffin. "She looks at peace," he said softly.

Martha's hand twitched a bit of lace at Phyllis's collar, folding it up to cover her neck. There had been no autopsy, and no comments about the woman's death. Martha told them about Phyllis's cat that sometimes scratched viciously, and that explanation was accepted for the twin punctures below her ear.

"I'll be leaving town next week," Mr. D'Aggacy told the ladies as he escorted them out of the funeral home. "I'm afraid I've been called away, on pressing. . ." he hesitated, "family business."

Agatha fussed and twittered, but Martha barely heard her. Martha's mind was on the warmth and light she'd find at the end of this evening, when she stopped in to say hello to Thomas and his family. Preoccupied, she never heard Mr. D'Aggacy say where he was going—if he said at all. And she was surprised at her mixed feelings about his departure.

"There are only shades of gray," she whispered as she piloted herself and Agatha through the quiet streets.

"What, dear?" Agatha said, turning from the window.

"I just said," Martha sighed. "I just said, there are only so many cards to play, Agatha. But hearts must always trump in the end."

SPEARFINGER

multitude of birds flit
from limb to limb in the shadowy depths of a forest in what will someday
be called North Carolina. The towering chestnuts, oaks, pines, maples,
and pecans play host to dozens of squirrels that run and chatter like children the day before a holiday. The forest floor is deeply padded with year
upon year of fallen leaves, rotting branches, and trailing vines. If one
steps quietly—if one knows how—he can pass through the trees virtually unnoticed.

A sudden quiet falls across the inhabitants of this primordial forest.
Sensing danger, they either freeze in their tracks or flee to a place of
refuge. They have detected sounds no mere human ear could pick up.

A high-pitched giggle breaks the hush, and five children, released
from the self-imposed silence, scamper beneath the trees.

"You can't catch me!" taunts one, and they all begin to run, scrambling for the edge of the forest and the bank that leads to a cool stream
beyond. One child, the youngest, is left behind, her short legs struggling
valiantly to keep up.

"Don't leave me," she shrieks. This provokes no response, and she
shudders, looking around at the still, still woods.

"I'll tell Mama," she hollers. This produces the desired reaction, and
soon her older brother circles around, back in sight, grabbing her up and
tickling her until she shrieks again.

"Stop, oh stop!" She picks herself up and begins to untangle leaves
from her tightly braided hair, pulling out strands in the process.

"Now you've mussed my hair," she complains, but her brother pulls her along behind him as he races for the stream bank and the company of friends.

"Spearfinger didn't get you that time, Rabbit?" teases one of the big girls as the two stragglers come into sight.

"Her flesh isn't tender enough!" howls another.

"Spearfinger doesn't care! Her finger's sharp enough to cut the toughest old hide!"

"Spearfinger got my uncle," asserts a solemn little boy, almost as small as Rabbit. "She took on the face of my auntie and hugged him tight. Next day, when my auntie got back, she got mad when my uncle didn't say hello. He thought he'd already seen her!"

"How long did it take him to die, Little Thunder?" asks Rabbit. The other children cluster around, too. Even though they've heard this and similar stories a hundred times, children never lose their appetite for fear. As long as it's safely contained in the past.

"He wasted away for nearly two seasons," Little Thunder declares. "I was only a baby, but my mama still cries. He was her favorite brother."

"Spearfinger!" screams a figure, rolling and sliding down the steep bank, straight at the children. They scream in reply and scatter.

The newcomer, practically grown at age thirteen, has come to gather up the children for the evening meal. They protest but at last agree to leave the stream with all its alluring promises of tadpoles, dragonflies, and other wonders. Sure enough, before they make their way to the clearing where their village waits, the sun has slid below the horizon and shadows play behind and before them. It gets dark sooner in the mountains. The shadows fall prematurely and longer, across the somber valleys of the Great Smoky Mountains.

They children edge a little closer to each other, not disdaining the warm hand of a friend to link them closer together.

"Spearfinger likes the dark," cackles the teenager who was sent to fetch them. "Slurp, slurp. Mmm. . .juicy little. . ." he reaches behind him with a sudden motion and snatches Rabbit's brother. "Liver!"

The children all shriek, but now that it's dark there's a thin edge of panic that wasn't there in the daylight. They can't make it back to the warmth of firelight and family fast enough to suit their apprehensive hearts.

The familiar lines of the stockade enclosing their village lay just beyond the fields of maize, sweet potato, and other crops tended by the women and girls of the village. Several families sit together and eat their evening meal: roasted chestnuts, plump ears of corn, and fresh-killed venison.

"A warrior from the Wild Potato clan died last week," says Kuwa, Little Thunder's mother, after tearing off a chunk of meat and handing it to the boy.

"Snakebite?"

"No, he'd been wasting for a while." She directs her gaze toward the children. "I believe your friend's mother, Echuta, found a honeybee's tree today. Go see!" All four children jumped up and ran toward the cooking fire across the village.

"They think it was Utlunta," she continues after the children are out of earshot. "He had seen a strange old woman on the trail when he was tracking a deer, but of course he thought nothing of it. He directed her toward a strawberry patch, thought she was visiting someone in his clan."

"Did he feel anything? Did she get close?"

"You know Spearfinger doesn't have to get too close. That finger is sharp enough, they say you never feel a thing. Of course, he didn't notice any marks. But there's no reason why that warrior had to die. He was young and strong."

"We'll have to keep an eye out for her."

"Yes," says Kuwa. "And make sure the children stay close together. It's a shame they're not even safe right next to the village."

Little Thunder's father snorts and shifts on his haunches. He doesn't believe this foolishness. It could have been a deadly spiderbite or something else that killed that warrior. Kuwa sees signs of Utlunta everywhere since her brother died.

The next morning, a big party of girls and women leaves the village, carrying baskets and a torch. It is time to gather chestnuts, and building a fire in the leaves below the chestnut trees will bring the succulent nuts down like rain.

"I don't like doing this when we've just heard again about Utlunta," whispers Kuwa to Rabbit's mother. "She could see the smoke from miles away and find one of us alone."

"Well, I won't turn my back on you," jokes Tsisquga. "She might choose to disguise herself like you, if she's smart. Then she could get all the liver she wanted, because everybody trusts *you*."

"It's not funny," insists Kuwa.

"I know," says Tsisquga, draping a friendly arm across the other's shoulders.

"Don't," mutters Kuwa, and she pulls away from the other woman's touch and keeps her distance all day long. Everyone is a little nervous because Kuwa's story from the Wild Potato Clan spread rapidly through the village, and the thought of Spearfinger's long, stony index finger, sharpened to an evil point, grated on everyone's nerves. Not one woman would leave the group, not even to go into the bushes to relieve herself. Everyone walks in pairs.

After working for a few hours, the same band of five children slips off to hunt for berries. Rabbit, as usual, tends to lag behind, but her big brother keeps urging her to keep up.

When they find a patch of sweet, ripe blackberries, they gorge themselves, laughing at the spectacle of dark-purple juice staining faces and hands. "I'm thirsty!" yells one, and they all take off in the direction of a little stream they'd crossed earlier.

"Wait," screams Rabbit, running wildly. Just as she crests the little hill above the stream, she trips across a root and sprawls, sobbing, her mouth full of leaves and twigs. She hears a noise to her left and swings recklessly around to meet the danger, but it's only a squirrel, watching her curiously. She laughs, relieved. Standing up, she brushes off and trots down the hill.

"Little girl," a voice quavers.

Rabbit freezes in her tracks, not quite believing she heard the voice.

"Little girl, come here and let me fix your braids." The voice is soft and coaxing.

Just then, Rabbit's brother comes running up the hill to grab her arm and pull her to the streambed. "What are you doing?" he demands crossly. "You shouldn't wander away like that."

Rabbit starts to protest that she had been left behind and to tell him about the voice she heard, but she soon gets caught up in their games and forgets the menace she thought she heard in the old woman's voice.

Later that night, her mother sets her down and begins to dress her hair with nimble fingers, singing funny little songs as she works. This reminds Rabbit, and she decides to entrust her mother with her tale.

"Mama, an old lady asked me to let her fix my braids today," Rabbit starts, as casually as she can. But her mother's hands tense up, pulling Rabbit's scalp much too tightly, before she grasps the child's shoulders and whirls her around to face her.

"Who?" she asks sharply.

"Ow, you're hurting me." Tsisquga loosens her grip slightly. "I don't know, Mama. It was on the hill, just past the berry patch."

"Were you alone? Did she touch you? What did she look like?"

Rabbit begins to be afraid all over again now. She had almost forgotten the terror of the moment, but her mother's alarm is contagious. "No, Mama, I ran away. I didn't even look at her, maybe she wasn't even there." Rabbit begins to cry, and immediately her mother softens, hugs her close, and rocks her gently, crooning those funny little songs about hedgehogs and buzzards and bees.

That night, Rabbit is tucked up safely in her blanket, while her parents and their friends play games by the light of the fire outside the hut.

The stones rattle and fall on the packed earth, and the cheers and howls of winners and losers punctuate Rabbit's drowsy half-sleep.

"Ten! I win!" shouts one, as he adds up the symbols showing on the stone's face.

"I heard some more about Utlunta," whispers Kuwa, disregarding her husband's glare.

Tsisquga shakes her head, more to dislodge the sensations of danger than to deny her friend the pleasure of telling a story.

"I heard something today, too," boomed Yanu, a warrior nearly past his prime. "You remember Golanv, who broke his head open at the last game of 'little war'? Seems he got his heart broken next—his girl went off with some other buck—so he went way off, hunting. He was in the woods a long, long way from here—beyond the beginnings of the river—and was perched up in a tree, waiting for a deer. He heard a noise, and before long, he saw an old, old woman wandering through the woods. She had a funny-looking hand—her fingers weren't right, he said. And she was going through the woods, singing 'Liver, I eat it. Su-su-sai. Liver, I eat it. Su-su-sai.'"

"What nonsense," spits Little Thunder's father. "Women's tales and nonsense! I guess you just don't have anything better to do than spin tales and gossip!" He stands up, disgusted, and stalks off. Kuwa shrugs and holds her palms up.

"I need to tell you something," Tsisquga says softly. "But I think we need to hold a council."

First thing next morning, all the adults gather in the meeting hall, while the children are watched by two old grandmothers, too old to help make decisions. Rabbit's mother tells her story, and after much discussion, a plan is decided upon. On the trail leading from Chilhowee Mountain to the river, all the women and warriors will dig a great pit. Then they will somehow lure Utlunta down the path. Once she is trapped in the pit, the clan's warriors could kill her.

"Maybe we might catch some deer in that pit," grumbles Little Thunder's father. But he digs, like everyone else. Even the children help haul baskets of dirt to the garden patches, so the trail won't be marked by signs of digging.

"What's all this fuss about?" asks Guque querulously. "I can't be expected to keep up with all these little busy squirrels forever." The children, when they aren't helping their parents, dart around and behind the old grandmother until she's dizzy.

The pit is finally completed and camouflaged with leaves and branches to look like part of the trail. Rabbit and Little Thunder, holding hands tightly, creep behind the warriors who keep watch.

"Someone's coming," whispers a warrior. As the figure comes into sight, Rabbit draws in her breath. "It's Guque!" she hisses. "We can't let her fall, she'll get hurt!" Rabbit stands up, just as the old woman reaches the edge of the pit.

"Watch out, Grandmother!" she shouts, but it is too late. The old woman falls like a stone, and as the children and warriors rush down from their hiding spot, they hear a terrible wailing and thrashing from the bottom of the pit.

"That's not Guque!" shouts a warrior. Inside the pit, grimacing in fury, is a creature who bears only the slightest resemblance to a human being. Her skin is gray, not quite leathery, but tough-looking—almost like stone. "Get your bow!"

The warriors shoot arrow after arrow, sacrificing tips that took many precious hours to form. Each arrowhead meets her skin and shatters, stone against stone. Rabbit and Little Thunder watch, openmouthed, as the creature hurls back curse after curse.

"I ate your uncle's liver, boy!" she shrieks, directing her bile against Little Thunder. "Yours would be tasty, too!"

The birds of the forest had all gotten quiet at the noise of battle, but suddenly, a blue jay swoops, screeching angrily. Then another bird, a mockingbird, dives toward the creature's head, as if to attack it. She screeches too, angrily, but still unafraid. Above the pit, on a branch that sways with the battle's wind, a titmouse sings with all her might. "Unahu, unahu, unahu," she warbles urgently.

"Heart," cries Rabbit. "That means 'heart'! Shoot for her heart!"

The warriors load their bows again and shoot at the creature's chest. But this only makes her laugh mightily and scrabble for a handhold, trying to climb out of the pit.

A valiant little chickadee drops down into the pit, landing on her right hand, the hand with the long, thin finger like a spear. "Get off of me," she screams. "You nasty creature!" She shakes her hand, and her fear is evident now, but the chickadee will not be dislodged.

"Shoot her hand!" Little Thunder screams, holding his side as if to shield his liver from her covetous gaze. The hunters load and shoot again, loosing a storm of arrows, all rushing toward her fierce right hand.

At last, Spearfinger falls, writhing and clutching her hand in pain. Whatever kind of a monster she was, her heart was closest to her terrible weapon, her mighty spearfinger, which cuts so quickly her victims never feel the pain.

Even today, the chickadee, Tsikilili, is known as the truthteller. If you see her perched, singing, near the house of a man on a journey, it means the man will soon return safe. And if you see her perched on the hand of a harmless old lady, Rabbit and Little Thunder might just whisper some good advice over your shoulder: "Run!"

GEORGIA DREAMS

he field behind the little white clapboard house stretched, to a twelve-year-old's eyes, forever. And so did its possibilities. The tall grass was always in motion, sometimes swelling and cresting like the restless sea, sometimes dancing mischievously in the fall breezes. Even in the stillest, hottest days of August, when the whole world seemed suspended in a solution of viscous, liquid heat, the grasses moved ever so slightly, as if ruffled gently by a huge, unseen hand.

To the twins, that field sometimes became the depths of the ocean, harboring creatures too deliciously horrible to be exposed to the light of day. Or sometimes it was the plains of the dinosaurs, where the children roamed in fear of footsteps that made the earth tremble. Or sometimes the children pretended to be rabbits, scampering innocently from bank to brush and back again, pursuing their little wild dreams.

In the summer when school hours no longer held them, the twins would play from the time their mother left for work until nearly bedtime, creeping into the house at odd times to scavenge a single slice of bread or a piece of bologna, always alert to the sound of the TV that held their grandfather captive. When he began to hoist his massive frame from his chair to investigate the little noises they made as they scrabbled through the cupboards, they would slip out the kitchen door, heedlessly letting the screen slap back into the frame.

Sometimes he would stand on the stoop and shake his fist at them, but once outside, they were safe. He could not follow them into the grasses. Into their dreams.

Tina ran her finger along the spines of the books, mentally reviewing each of them as she touched them. There were only thirty titles on the library shelf marked "Travel" and she had read each of them. Cover to cover. Even the 1978 edition of *Europe On $5 A Day*, which really, she thought, belonged on the history shelves, not here. With a sigh, she pulled *Venice* off the shelf and took it to the library table. She knew the meager text by heart, but the pictures still held the power to pull her in, make her lose herself in the twisting, turning alleyways endlessly cut through by bands of water. Sometimes the water she studied was as black and unrevealing as an oil slick, and sometimes the light played on it, creating a brilliant palette of blues and greens, silvers and grays. As she absorbed the photographs, she could nearly feel the cobblestones under her feet and smell the sour, slightly fishy odor of a city by the sea.

Tina jumped when the librarian touched her shoulder.

"It's nearly closing time, Tina," the woman said kindly. "Better pick one out and head over to the store to meet your mom."

Tina closed the book and returned it to the shelf. She felt unsettled, uneasy in her body and with her thoughts. One minute she wanted to be as far from this little town in Georgia as she could get—Alaska, say, or Russia. But the next minute she felt like a little baby again, wanting desperately for her mother to greet her after school with a glass of milk and smiling inquisitions about her teacher and her day. Her skin didn't seem to fit, and her mind seemed to skip in every direction at once. Pulling another book off the shelf, without even glancing at the title, she slouched to the checkout desk and gave the librarian a wan little smile.

"See you tomorrow, Tina," the librarian said brightly after she'd stamped the book and handed it over. Tina said nothing, just gave a little half-wave and stuffed the book into her backpack on her way out the door.

The sun was just setting behind the high school when Tina trudged along the sidewalk toward the Piggly Wiggly where her mother had worked since the divorce.

"You ever been to Venice?"

The voice seemed to come from nowhere, and Tina whirled around to confront a tall man she'd never seen before.

"No," she said suspiciously. She hurried her steps. The Pig was only half a block away.

"I lived there once."

Almost without thought, Tina's pace faltered a bit.

"Those pictures don't do it justice."

His voice was soft, with a trace of an accent. She snuck another glance at him, over her shoulder, and relaxed imperceptibly. He reminded her, a little, of her dad. His eyes were green, and his hair was just a week or so overdue for a trim.

"My name is Paul Marriot. I'll be teaching geography over at the high school starting next semester. Are you a student there?"

Tina laughed. "I'm only in the sixth grade. But thanks."

"I'd love to tell you about Venice sometime. If you really want to know a place, you have to live there. Don't you think so, too?"

Tina's stride had slowed considerably, and now she stopped completely, to consider what he'd said. She spoke slowly, carefully. It seemed an important question.

"I think, maybe, you can see a place more clearly when you first get there. Once you become familiar with it, your eyes just sort of, I don't know, miss things."

His eyes had focused intensely on her heart-shaped face as she first spoke, noting the soft, fine strands of blond hair just turning to brown. But before her sentence was finished, she felt his eyes flicker past her, to the mouth of the alleyway beside the grocery store. All at once her instincts began to shriek, and her brain sent frantic signals to her legs. But just like in a nightmare, her muscles were frozen stiff, and his hand clasped over her mouth too quickly to allow the scream rising in her throat to escape.

Although she struggled in his hands as he pulled her around to the back side of the dumpster, he easily managed to restrain her. He was, after all, three inches over six feet, and this child was slight, all arms and legs like so many twelve year olds. As he bent towards her throat, her eyes rolled back into her head. She'd fainted. His nose wrinkled slightly. She'd also voided her bladder, an unpleasant side effect of fright.

Paul's teeth touched the soft skin of her neck, and as always, he was filled, buoyed up, by a wash of hope. Perhaps this time his hunger would be filled. Perhaps this child had what he needed. As the warm, thick liquid drifted over his tongue and down his throat he shuddered, on the verge of some feeling too complex, too terrible, and too joyous to name.

Tina's eyelids fluttered. Behind them, her mind was creating scenes of the world she would never see. Quickly, instantly, her mind's eye flew through the streets of Paris, lingering over the square-cut chestnut trees of Luxembourg Gardens, then swooped southwards to the city of canals. As a curtain of gray began to creep slowly down over the scene, her heart danced at the sight of the water, the fractured pieces of turquoise, teal, deep purple, flashing green. She could hear the soft plish, plish of an oar cutting smoothly through the water, and then everything was black.

He was almost sated, almost back to that point of simple joy when he felt the pulse of life slow and finally still. He sat back on his heels, holding the limp and lifeless form, and felt the tears slip down his face, scalding a trail. Somehow, he'd miscalculated again. This one did not have what he needed.

Carefully, almost reverentially, he placed the body into the dumpster. He used a tissue from the bookbag to wipe his face and hands, and then tossed the bag in the dumpster, too. He sauntered slowly out of the other end of the alley, into an evening that was washed to the west with pale pinks and vivid blues.

Infrequently, the distant family who owned the field would send someone to mow it. The twins would stand at the edge of the field, holding hands, feeling dispossessed as the tractor roared its way across and back and forth over their haven. Once the intruder was gone, they would return, now with the freedom to spin and twirl and fly across the space. They would get so dizzy that they would collapse, breathless and laughing, onto the hard little stalks remaining.

The stubble poked them, painfully, but it was a pain preferable to the wrath of the old man inside. When he called them, insisting on a meal or a bath, they would lie quite still in the devastated grass, their arms entwined. After his shouts died away, they could hear the roar of the log trucks on the road bordering the far side of the field. Their gears were clashing and grinding as they toiled their way between dwindling forest and hungry sawmill.

Heather tugged her ball cap down more firmly over the nest of hair twisted on top of her head. She'd spent the last two hours on the edge of the little county airport, lying in the grass and watching the tiny two-, four-, and six-seaters land and take off, land and take off, as businessmen headed to Savannah or Atlanta. A few lucky souls were taking flying lessons, and that was the hangar Heather was heading toward. She had called, when she was ten, to learn that flying lessons were an impossible $65 an hour, and you had to be sixteen to fly alone.

But that wasn't to say that you couldn't learn things on the ground before you start. And, who knows, she thought defensively, they might even let me sort of work my way through. I can clean up, wash the planes, or whatever in exchange for lessons.

Flying was a compulsion for her. Her mother—back in the days when she still noticed she had a daughter, before Tim went off the deep end—used to laugh that Heather was reaching for birds out of the sky on the drive home from the hospital. When the air show came to town, Heather cajoled her father to shell out the twenty bucks for a brief ten minute ride. During that ten minutes, Heather had known for certain that she was as close to heaven as she'd ever come on this earth.

Her dad had said something then—she was ten that year — about flying lessons. But then her brother Tim discovered pot and then cocaine, and Heather might as well have been on the moon for all the attention her parents paid her. When she'd dared to mention the flying lessons again, just after her eleventh birthday, her father's face got all stony and her mother had teared up.

"Honey, this program Timmy's in, it costs a lot of money," her mother had explained through her tears. "We just don't have anything to spare for something like flying lessons."

Now she was twelve, Tim was into his third recovery program, and she'd better start sprouting wings or something if she ever wanted to get back up into the air.

"You like to fly?"

Heather narrowed her eyes at this tall guy who'd sort of materialized beside her.

"See that little Ovation over there?" He pointed to a little four-seater, white with racy blue stripes. He didn't seem to notice that she hadn't answered him. Or maybe he didn't mind. "That's my baby. Too bad I don't get to fly her as often as I'd like."

"Wow. It's a Mooney, right? With 280 horses and a cruise speed as fast as a turbocharged engine?"

He nodded, smiling a little. "Yeah, 190 knots at 5,000 feet. Takes about 15 gallons an hour. She'll stay up for six hours without a refill."

"It's beautiful." Heather's heart ached. Her throat closed up over the words she knew she couldn't ever ask. But to her amazement, he spoke them for her.

"I'll need a little help this weekend, cleaning her up and getting her ready for a little trip I'm taking. Why don't you see if your parents would let you help me, and I could give you a ride or two in exchange?"

Heather's eyes sparkled. She let out a low whoop and turned to give the man a high five. Just as his big hand touched her palm, she sensed something awry in his manner or tone. She began to pull back, a cry forming in her throat, but he grasped her hand in his and pulled her close, clamping his other hand tightly against her lips.

Paul carried her easily over a little rise, into the field where she'd lain and watched the planes earlier. Her eyes were wide and panicky, and she struggled mightily to get away. At one point, she sunk her teeth deeply into the meat of his palm, causing him to cry out and slap her angrily.

Pinning her hands painfully behind her back with one big hand, Paul leaned over toward her neck, his sharp fangs searching instinctively for the throbbing vein that would, he hoped, end his torment. As he began to drink, he again felt that expectation of redemption that every episode brought. He felt an overriding sense of confidence that this girl, this time, could fill that aching void within. Blood spilled from her neck into the soft earth below, and he moaned in anticipation.

Heather's fingers twitched, brushing the grass behind her back. In her mind, she swooped and soared above the hills, held up only by the power of her own arms. No engine noise interfered, no metal came between her and the air she cut through in her flight. She was gliding, elevated far above the tiny town and fields below. Her family were little specks of color, her mother's tears and her father's anger only a memory as she flew higher, higher, higher still. Soon gray clouds worked their way between the land and her ascending form, obscuring her view and then slowly, quietly, turning into blackness.

Paul felt the last bit of life drain from the girl's slender form and threw back his head, moaning in anguish. This time, he'd felt it. He'd tasted it. That unnameable, undecipherable joy that only comes with twelve-year-old dreams. He'd had it on his tongue, almost had it in his heart, when she died. Now it was too late, and he could only go on searching.

As they slept, the twins dreamed the same dreams, just as in the daytime they could exchange a glance and know, without a word, what the other was thinking. Their mother insisted they sleep in separate beds. The house had only one bedroom, and the twins usually crept into the same bed after their mother's breathing became light and regular. They curled up, nesting like spoons, arms and legs tangled like kudzu. As they slept, you could see the bizarre symmetry of their features side-by-side. Although they were fraternal, not identical twins, they bore a startling resemblance to each other.

One morning their mother left for work early, without waking them. Their grandfather arrived and crept into their room, muttering. When he saw their limbs entwined, he let out an angry roar.

"You slut!" he screamed, and four green eyes popped open in instant recognition of danger. "You little tramp!" His hand, big and calloused and not slowed at all by age, swooped down toward the motionless forms on the bed. "You're just like your mother!"

With a smoothness born of practice, the twins slid from the bed and away from the threatening hand. Snatching willy-nilly at clothes scattered around the room, they fled out the door, through the kitchen, and bolted to the field beyond the door.

Shannon wiggled, smoothing the denim miniskirt down over her hips. She checked her hair in the mirror and winced when she heard her mother screech.

"Shannon, I'm leaving *right now*, so get your butt in here!"

When the girl walked into the living room, her mother gasped. "Just where do you think you're going in that getup, young lady?"

Shannon plopped down on the sofa and studied one long, lacquered nail. "You said you wanted me to go to church," she drawled.

Her mother laughed, a short, bitter sound. "Not like that, you're not. I don't want people to think I let my girl walk around showing her little tush. At twelve, for God's sake." She popped Shannon lightly on the thigh. "Go change."

The girl got up as slowly as she dared and sashayed to her bedroom door.

"Damn," her mother said. "It's 7:30 already, and I'm supposed to lead the women's study group. I don't have time to wait for you to change."

Shannon turned, again moving with excruciating slowness.

Her mother sighed. "Stay here, then. Don't open the door to anybody. Don't you have homework to do?" Without waiting for a reply, she hurried out the door, pulling it shut and locked with a bang.

Shannon watched her mother leave through the big plate-glass window, barely moving the elaborate window coverings to peer out to the driveway. Five minutes later, she'd put on her little rabbit jacket and stuffed a twenty (stolen from her mom's purse) into the pocket. She pulled the door shut softly, as if to avoid waking any ghosts that might linger in the still house. Or perhaps it was her dreams she didn't want to stir.

She walked along the shoulder of the road, trying not to twist an ankle on the uneven edge of the asphalt or slip down into the drainage ditch which beckoned bleakly below. It didn't take long for a car to pull alongside.

"Need a ride?"

Shannon bent over, straining her eyes to make out the shadowy face of the driver. He didn't look too old or too creepy, so she shrugged her shoulders and hopped in. Her skirt crept up a little too far on her thighs, and she tugged at it uselessly.

"My name's Paul. Paul Marriot."

She looked over at him in some interest. His accent was kind of cute, she thought.

"I'm Shannon."

"Where are you headed, Shannon?"

She shrugged again, staring out at the dark countryside unrolling in front of the swiftly moving car.

"I grew up near here."

She shrugged for the third time and, as she'd done before, began to wonder why she'd gotten into this particular car, on this particular night. What if, she wondered, I'd put on that stupid-looking jumper Mom loves so much?

"You want a drink?" He offered her a bottle tucked inside a brown paper bag and she took it, downing a healthy shot before handing it back.

This beats church any day, she thought as the liquor coursed warmly through her blood. Bunch of dumb hypocrites, worried about clothes and cars, she thought to herself.

The car was beginning to slow and Shannon, alert, rested her hand on the door handle. She'd jumped out of cars before. She knew how to take care of herself.

Paul pulled the car into a side road and stopped, examining the girl by the dim, greenish glow of the instrument panel. At first he'd thought she was too old, but he could see by the faint roundness of her cheeks, the slender, almost shapeless form of her calves, that this was still a child.

"Keep your hands to yourself, Bud," she said, trying valiantly to sound bored, not scared. Just as she decided to make her escape, and her fingers curled around the comforting cold metal of the door latch, she heard an odd metallic "clunk." The door latch pulled out, but the door did not swing open, and with a sickening rush she knew he'd engaged the power door locks.

"Don't," she warned, but he was reaching for her, enfolding her with his oversized hands.

He felt a storm of sweet love overtake him as he leaned over her neck, just barely skimming the surface of her skin with his teeth. This one, he thought, is the right one. This one will be my salvation. And he was filled with a gratitude so immense he nearly cried. Because this little rabbit would save him from his indescribable loneliness, his incalculable pain.

As his fangs bit deep into her neck, Shannon's lips moved. She felt arms enclosing her, hands so big and strong and warm that she felt invulnerable, beyond any sorrow or pain. Her mouth curved up into a smile as she called out in her dreams, "Ah, there you are. You look just like I always imagined!" Shannon was cradled in light, and love, and peace, which was a soft dove-gray and faded slowly, kindly, into black.

Paul hurled the pliable, still-warm corpse from his arms, staggering from the car and into the fields beyond the road. "No," he cried. "NO!"

His hopes had ebbed away with the life force of this girl, and his despair was heavier than he could endure. He fell into the stubble of the newly mown field, sobbing, heedless of the stalks that gouged his flesh before he crumpled back into the dirt.

This time, Grandfather's anger had propelled him out the door and after the twins, screaming in wordless rage as he reached for their angular frames. They scrambled out of his reach, but the field had no tall grass to shield them. No safe corners to screen them from his fury.

They stumbled and staggered, the three of them, through the stalks and clods, nearly an acre, before the twins reached the side of the logging road. The old man, a crazy grin on his face, careened up the slight embankment and reached for the little girl.

"C'mere, you little slut," he hissed.

She hesitated, glancing in confusion from her brother to her grandfather to the road and threw herself across the asphalt surface.

"Polly, no!" Her brother screamed, flinging his arms out to stop her, too late. A massive truck, heavy with pines still bleeding from their cuts, was thundering down the incline.

What was left was not much more than a dog would leave. Only a small scrap of pink, her flannel nighty, distinguished the child from any other roadkill. Dazed, the surviving twin reached out a finger to touch the spreading pool of blood.

"Polly?" he whimpered and touched his bloody finger to his lips.

MARRYING FOOL

 am an old man now and in many ways a fortunate one. But most of all, I count myself fortunate to have survived my thirty-seventh year. That is the year I came under the spell of a creature so consummately evil, she could have made the Devil himself blanch. In fact, she may be doing that even as I write.

It was the spring of 1850. I was in the prime of my life, new master of my father's plantation. I enjoyed a stable full of fine horses, the attention of the most beautiful belles across the county, and the companionship of my peers whenever I chose. As I surveyed my land one day, astride a particularly fine bay stallion, I chanced to see my neighbor's carriage flying helter-skelter down the road. It was unlike George Rouett to drive his horses so cruelly, and I craned my neck to see who held the reins. I saw only a glimpse of fine white lawn, a flash of black hair, almost blue in the sunlight, and pale, pale arms.

My curiosity was piqued. The best way to find out what was going on at Seven Oaks was, of course, through servants' gossip, so I asked my body servant that evening if he had heard of anything unusual at the neighbors'. He hadn't, so I went to bed with my curiosity unsatisfied.

The next day was taken up by a consultation with the overseer, some unpleasant business involving the sale of some servants, and various other tasks. I was unable to ride over to Seven Oaks to see my neighbor and inquire about the identity of the mysterious raven-haired beauty. As I prepared for bed, I resolved to ride out early in the morning to visit George Rouett.

The day dawned clear, but with an ominous line of black, brooding clouds on the western horizon. We were preparing to plant our summer crop and a driving rainstorm would not be fortuitous, but all I could do was shrug. The weather was beyond my control. I didn't know, as I cantered slowly across the fields toward Seven Oaks, that I was heading toward a force much more powerful than a mere thunderstorm. A force that would render me as helpless as the old, broken-down mules that plowed the fields of my plantation.

"George!" I shook his hand as he came into the front hall of his house. He, like me, had inherited his father's plantation, house, and style of living. We were lucky, but we had only the most vague of ideas about how others lived. We were raised to be what we were. Perhaps if we'd had a broader sense of the world, this story would be far less tragic.

"I have the most incredible news, Thomas!" He led me to the library, talking all the way. "I went to Mobile to visit my cousins and arrange for some shipments, and you won't believe what happened to me!" He stopped, grasping my shoulder. "Thomas, I fell in love."

I drew back in mock horror. "Anything but that, George!"

He was deadly serious. "Wait until you meet her, Thomas. Words just can't describe her. She's charming, intelligent, warm, and caring. She's. . ."

Just then, the door to the library flew open. A woman as radiant as the rising sun skipped out, laughing. She clasped George's arm with slender, delicate fingers and pinned me with eyes an extraordinary shade of green. The first moment I met her, they were the clear, glowing green of sunlight through a canopy of spring foliage.

"My ears are burning, George!" The musical cadence of her voice was a perfect match for her flawless features. "Introduce me, please, and do stop talking behind my back!"

George beamed, looking a little foolish, I suppose, as only men who are hopelessly besotted can, but I was so dazzled I scarcely noticed.

He bowed to me with a little flourish. "May I present my wife, Elizabeth Rouett."

I bent low over her hand. Behind her, I caught a glimpse of a servant scurrying out of the library, doubled over as if in pain. The sight struck an incongruous note, but the significance never dawned on me until it was too late.

"George, Mrs. Rouett, may I be the first in the county to offer you my warmest congratulations?"

"Oh, do call me Elizabeth," she said, drawing me along behind her into the library. "We'll all be such good friends, I'm sure."

We did become close, spending evenings at cards until way past midnight, riding out together when the weather was fine, careening across the fields, Elizabeth with her hair streaming out behind her like a banner. We feasted together, great banquets of roasted beef, fowl, and ham and rich red wines. I marveled at Elizabeth's voracious appetite. I often saw her tear into a roast so rare it would have turned my stomach. But her dainty white teeth, framed so prettily by ripe, crimson lips and contrasting so sharply with her hair of spun sable, made me forgive such small savageries.

Before the weather grew oppressive, I noticed a change in George. He became quiet and tired more easily, withdrawing from our card games earlier and earlier and declining to join us on our wild gallops through the countryside. One evening I confronted Elizabeth with George's waning health.

"I'm worried about him, Elizabeth," I said frankly. "I know you haven't known him long, but really, this is most unusual for him. He had far more stamina than I just three months ago."

Her remarkable eyes changed so rapidly I drew in my breath. From the clear, innocent emerald of spring leaves, they turned into the murky, angry green of a stagnant creek. Then, just as quickly, they changed back, and she smiled sweetly at me with her small, strong teeth showing clearly.

"I'm afraid he finds marriage a bit tiresome, dear Thomas," she pouted. I fought an urge to kiss her hard enough to consume that expression, those lips. I was at once ashamed of my ready passion for the wife of a friend, yet aflame with the idea that she might be receptive to it.

I stood up abruptly. If there are angels, they were looking over me that night. "I must go, Elizabeth," I said, and took my leave. It was, I realized, quite rude, but also quite the best I could manage and still keep my friendship with George alive.

Despite my best intentions, my friendship with George was doomed to an untimely end. He died before July was out. I only saw him one other time, on the veranda early one morning. He was so gaunt, his pallor so pronounced that I exclaimed aloud in dismay.

"My God, man, what's happened to you?"

He murmured something about a malady of the blood, but so softly I could barely decipher his words. Elizabeth swirled out, in a flurry of petticoats and jet-black curls, to guide him back into the house. I went on to the overseer's house, to discuss a question of boundaries that had come up between our two plantations. I was strangely disturbed by the sight of George but trusted that Elizabeth and his servants, many of whom had grown up with him, would give him the best possible care.

Of course everyone in the county came to the funeral. His grieving widow was resplendent in black, and many of the men who gathered on the veranda for a cigar after the meal commented on her unusual beauty. Some were even laying odds on how long she would remain unmarried, but such talk disgusted me. I hurried back into the house.

"Dear Thomas, how shall I ever get along without George to take care of me?" She held my arm softly, looking up at me. Those remarkable eyes were highlighted by thick, black lashes glittering with teardrops. My defenses crumbled, and I again fell into such a storm of passion that my brain could not find words for my mouth to speak. Then, as before, I was so mortified by my animal instincts with my friend not even cold in his grave that I muttered incoherently and fled out the door.

Three months later, I was again overlooking my fields when George's carriage came bolting down the road to his house. I was afraid Elizabeth had lost control of the horses when I saw her slender arms wielding the whip, crying for more speed, and heard the answering cry of laughter from the figure at her side. When I queried my body servant that night, he knew, this time, what was happening at Seven Oaks.

"She done got married again, suh." He shook his head, disapproval emanating from him in waves. He would never criticize her with words, but his eloquence was impressive all the same.

I pressed him for details, but he would say no more, his lips compressed tightly as if to hold in his opinion. I, too, was a bit surprised at the haste of her new marriage, but the plantation and its slaves required a man's firm hand to run smoothly. Or at least, that was my opinion.

I saw Elizabeth's second husband only once. He was riding out with her, along our mutual boundaries on the western side of my property. He sat on his horse like a sack of potatoes and tipped his ridiculous top hat to me when Elizabeth introduced us. He was thin, painfully so, which reminded me of my final encounter with George. He, too, was exceptionally pale, but Elizabeth was as vibrant and glowing as always. Perhaps even more so. We exchanged a few pleasantries and a promise to get together, but my heart wasn't in it. I suppose he could sense that.

In December, Elizabeth's second husband died. I shivered when I heard the news. For some odd reason, the thought of her sharp, brilliant teeth flashed through my mind. But the holiday season was packed full of social engagements, and I pushed thoughts of the widow Elizabeth far into the recesses of my mind. I danced night after night with slender, sweet young girls, each of them as pliable as a honeysuckle vine in my arms and just as eager to twine their fortune to my own. But none of them held my attention. My dreams were thick with clouds of raven hair and punctuated with eyes of glowing green.

It was spring again, and I was thirty-eight. Had my mother been alive, she would have been pressing me into marriage to produce heirs for our family name. But she was not, and I continued in my solitary lifestyle. I often rode along the slight ridge that divided the Rouett plantation from my own, and my thoughts would turn to Elizabeth. I knew, from my own servants' gossip, that her slaves were not receiving the kind of guidance they required to make Seven Oaks a thriving plantation.

There were many mutters of strange goings-on, and my manservant hinted that Elizabeth was not well-liked. Of course, any master—or mistress—who took a stern hand with the servants would not be popular, but it always helps to have a lenient mistress to offset a harsh overseer or a strict master. I myself indulged my servants too often, as my overseer constantly reminded me, but I was born soft-hearted and couldn't help myself.

What a grand plantation it would make, I mused as I rode one spring evening, if Seven Oaks and my own property were joined together. Perhaps I should call on Elizabeth.

As if summoned by my thoughts, the Rouett carriage came hurtling down the road towards the house. Driving it, recklessly as usual, was Elizabeth. Beside her sat a man about my age. I stared, astonished. Surely Elizabeth couldn't have found another husband so soon.

But she had. As Samuel tugged off my muddy boots, he told me in short, terse sentences about the preparations Elizabeth had ordered before leaving for Mobile a week ago. A feast was to be prepared, and the house servants dismissed to the quarters as soon as the bride and groom arrived. They would celebrate alone, and Elizabeth would wait upon her new husband herself.

I waited until Samuel left me to vent an extraordinary anger. I felt cheated. This beautiful, desirable woman should have become my wife. Should have become the mother of my children. I wanted to see those incredible green eyes in every light. I wanted to see them cloudy with desire. I threw my glass of brandy into the fireplace in my rage, and the liquor ignited with a roar. That calmed me somewhat, but I still summoned Samuel to me and ordered him to pack for a trip to Mobile. I was going to find a spouse of my own.

I came back from Mobile three weeks later, defeated and exhausted. I had seen and dismissed an inordinate number of young, hopeful women, all of them imminently suitable to become my partner. But none of them sparked more than a flicker of interest. They all seemed simpleminded ninnies or else to be masking a shrewish cast of character, making me wary of making a commitment. None of them had the essential ingredients I required in a wife. They were not, in short, Elizabeth Rouett.

I rode along the ridge the morning after my return, trying—and failing—to avoid thoughts of Elizabeth and her new husband. My eyes were drawn to George's mansion, with its graceful columns and sweeping veranda. Something black on the door caught my eye, and I drew in my breath in disbelief. A black crepe wreath hung on the door. The house was in mourning.

I spurred my horse unmercifully, driving him down the ridge and across the field to the house. I threw myself to the ground and flew up the stairs to pound on the door, nearly sobbing in my fear.

When Elizabeth opened the door, my sense of relief was so strong I didn't question the absence of the family's houseman. I held out my arms, and she moved into their circle, delicately touching her eyes with a black cambric handkerchief trimmed in fine black lace.

"Oh, it's been so horrible, Thomas," she cried. "It's like a nightmare. My dear husband, taken so cruelly, just one night after we returned."

"What happened, my dear?" I murmured into the crown of her head, hardly caring about the response.

"He just went to sleep and never woke up." She sniffed once or twice, bravely restraining her grief.

"Poor, poor dear," I said, stroking her hair. My fingers fairly tingled at this contact with my beloved. I scarcely knew what I said. I only knew that Providence, some grand force, seemed to be bringing the two of us together.

I did not propose that day. Samuel was so sullen as I prepared for bed that I had to question him about his mood. At first he merely shook his head, his lips compressed in his strangely expressive manner.

"Samuel," I said finally, exasperated. "You and I grew up together. I've known you since the day you were born. For God's sake, tell me what's wrong!"

"That woman's no good," he muttered. I saw him make the sign against the evil eye behind his back, and that made me angry.

"Dammit, that superstition foolishness has got to go, Samuel!" I exploded. "Doesn't your preacher tell you it's all nonsense?"

"He don't come but once a month," Samuel said quietly. "Servants over at Seven Oaks seen things they know is evil. It's that woman who needs a preacher, not me."

I lost control. I hit him. I'd never hit a servant before, much less my dear companion Samuel. He and I had been born a month apart. His mammy was my own. It was her chocolate-brown hands that smoothed my brow through countless illnesses. It was Samuel who had explored with me every nook and cranny of the land that was to become my own. But this time, I felt, he'd gone too far. To say that my Elizabeth was evil. Sometimes, I thought, I can almost believe that slaves have no souls. Samuel and the other slaves apparently could not feel the beauty, the goodness that personified Elizabeth, in body and in spirit.

"You may go." I dismissed Samuel coldly, thinking him lucky that I did not order him whipped. Now, as I remember that evening, I am more deeply ashamed of my behavior than of anything I have ever done, before or since. Samuel's mother had no medicine, no cool compress to fight the fever that was raging through me at that moment.

The next morning, my breakfast was late. When it arrived, it was stone cold. I suffered in silence. But when dinner appeared on my table and the potatoes were so raw they could not be cut, my anger erupted.

"What the hell is going on here?" I demanded of the little girl who serves at table. "Go get me that damn cook. Tell Samuel and Simon to get in here too."

She scurried off. Of course, all three servants denied that there was any kind of intentional mischief going on, but I knew differently. I seethed and sent them away. To top off a perfectly horrible meal, a servant from my aunt's household arrived with dreadful news. My aunt, my mother's favorite younger sister, had died unexpectedly. There was nothing I could do except pack and leave at once to attend the funeral.

I penned a hasty note to Elizabeth. I could not bring myself to openly ask for her hand, since she was so recently bereaved, but I did mention our longstanding friendship, begging her to come to me at any time for my counsel and obliquely requesting permission to call on her. I left the note with Simon, my houseman, to deliver, since Samuel would accompany me to my aunt's funeral.

I returned a week later, late in the evening, hoping to find some correspondence from my beloved. As I stretched out in my chair with a brandy and cigar, I asked Simon if there had been any reply to my letter. He stared stonily at the floor.

"Now, now, Simon," I said lazily. "I know how you all feel about the lady, but you'll have to get used to her." Over the past week, I had come to my senses, realizing that my servants were merely misguided children. They really knew no better.

"I plan to make her my wife," I said, gesturing with my cigar so that a halo of smoke wafted around my head.

"Suh, she already married."

"No, Simon, her husband died. In May." I puffed again, surveying the room and wondering if she would feel the need to make many changes to the interior. It might seem a little shabby, having been the home of a bachelor so long.

"Suh, she married a man fum N'Awlins las' week."

I flew out of my chair, dropping the cigar without thought on the varnished floorboards, grabbing Simon by the collar.

"You're mad!" I cried. "That's impossible! She couldn't have married again so soon. You lie, you worthless. . ."

Samuel had come up behind me and picked up the cigar that lay smoldering on the floor.

"It be true, suh," he said softly.

"I don't believe it! Saddle my horse, I'll go over there now! She'll see me, she'll have me, she loves me!" My anguish was brutal. But as I rode over the ridge and down to her home, the evening air cleared my head. How could she have married so soon? After I had held her, written to her of my affections? Anger at her fickle behavior began to dominate my thoughts. Samuel and Simon had no cause to lie to me about this. They knew a lie would be quickly discovered and punished just as swiftly. It was Elizabeth who deserved my wrath. Elizabeth who had betrayed me.

I turned and rode back to my house, unsaddled my horse and locked myself in the library. I proceeded to drink myself into a stupor, finally falling asleep with my head on the cold stone of the hearth. Samuel came in the next morning—using a key Simon had secreted away—with a pot of very strong, hot coffee.

"I heered a screech owl las' night," he volunteered, after decently waiting for me to finish my first cup. "I put a shovel in the fire so no one would die, but I believes it came from down at Seven Oaks anyways."

I gurgled a bit into my coffee cup. Samuel knows me well and took that as a signal to leave me alone. I went upstairs and slept until the sun went down and then summoned a maid to my room.

"Tell 'Becca I want some eggs," I told her. "And tell Samuel to come here and help me get dressed. I'm going out."

I could tell something was wrong as soon as I saw Samuel. "What's wrong?" I asked, as he gave my boots a quick shine.

"Dat woman," he muttered. "Her new husband daid."

"What woman?" My head was still fuzzy from the great quantities of brandy I'd consumed the night before.

"Seven Oaks," he said, not looking me in the eye.

I grabbed his arm as he turned to leave.

"What are you talking about?"

Samuel shrugged.

"I won't hurt you, I promise. Tell me what you've heard!"

"He dead this morning when Mary go to take him breakfas'," Samuel said. "Thass all I knows." He would not tell me any more, but I heard him talking with Simon as I headed out the front door.

"She ate his soul," Simon insisted in a whisper, polishing the silver tea set on the dining room sideboard with an old rag. Samuel lounged against the wall, chewing on a straw.

"Naw, if she wuz a witch, that red pepper Mary sprinkled would've kilt her."

"'Becca say the milk cows dried up over there," Simon continued.

Just then, my foot nudged a walking stick in the foyer and it fell over with a loud clatter. Samuel straightened up and came over to escort me out the door. I spent the evening playing cards with the LeMont twins, at Belle Arbor. My mind was not on the game, however, and I lost quite a bit of money before I took my leave.

My suspicions grew when I heard in August that Elizabeth Rouett had married again. This time, she married a man with property in Mississippi, but they remained in Alabama to care for Seven Oaks. The LeMont twins were amused at what they termed her "damnable luck" with husbands, but I had begun to see it as something far more diabolical than luck. When I heard that the man from Mississippi had died, also just days after the wedding, I rode over to Belle Arbor. I felt I had to discuss the matter with my peers.

Andre was coolly dismissive of my suspicions. "The lady is unlucky, Thomas," he said. "Have a drink."

"But this was her fifth husband," I protested.

"One or two of them were pretty old, I heard." Daniel Reynolds, whose father owned Magnolia Groves and couldn't grow a decent crop of cotton to save his life, had also come to take advantage of the LeMont hospitality.

"None of them was over forty, for God's sake!"

Andre surveyed me speculatively. "I hear you were pretty interested in the lady for a while, Thomas."

His brother barked with laughter. "Let's see how lucky Thomas is tonight!"

When Samuel told me Elizabeth had married her sixth husband, I wasn't surprised. No one knew—in the slave quarters, anyway—where this man had come from, but he did not enjoy the company of the beautiful Elizabeth long. He was dead before the week was out.

"But how did he die, Samuel?"

"Nobody knows, suh. There wasn't a mark on him. Mary said he looked white as a sheet, but that's all."

I resolved to find out for myself what was going on at Seven Oaks. I rode out that afternoon, grimly determined to discover what kind of evil had taken root at the plantation of my dead friend. As I trotted over the fields, thunder rolled in the distance. I suppressed a shiver, remembering Samuel's superstitious belief that the sound was made by the devil riding in his black chariot.

I dismounted in front of the house and tossed the reins lightly over the hitching post. When the heavy brass door knocker struck the plate, the door swung open and she stood there, as blithe and as arresting as the day I had first met her.

"Elizabeth." I took off my hat and followed her into the entrance hall. "I have to know what's going on here. My servants are telling the most absurd stories." Seeing her, I could not believe an evil thought had ever crossed her mind or furrowed that smooth, porcelain brow.

She turned and smiled at me. In the dim light of the shaded house, I could not tell if her eyes were that unbelievable clear green or the murky angry emerald. I could see, however, over her shoulder, the grand mahogany hat rack that had been the pride of George's father. I strained my eyes to see. I could make out the old, shabby straw hat George always wore when he was working outdoors. I saw the tall, shiny top hat Elizabeth's second husband had worn the one time I met him. I counted, with rising horror, four more hats, and my eyes turned to my own hat, which I had unthinkingly twisted into a shapeless mass.

"You murdered them," I whispered, incredulous at her bold display of trophies. "You killed them all, didn't you?"

Her only answer was mocking laughter, and I backed out of the house, afraid to say any more.

I went immediately to the sheriff and laid out the whole sordid tale. He listened politely and agreed to investigate. I went home, satisfied that I had done my duty as a good citizen. Of course the sheriff would heed my warnings. I was an influential citizen in the county.

A week later, I returned to the sheriff's office. He was evasive but soon admitted that he had not found any evidence of foul play.

"This is appalling! Six men have died, sir, six perfectly healthy, young men, and you refuse to do anything?"

He shrugged. There was not enough evidence to prosecute anybody, he pointed out, and he wasn't going to ruin the lady's reputation for nothing.

"Nothing?" I roared. "Nothing? Is George Rouett NOTHING?" Despite all my blustering, the sheriff was unmoved. The lady was, in his mind, completely innocent.

I began a crusade. I called on each and every one of my neighbors, to warn them of the evil creature in our midst. I may have overstated my case a bit or been too emphatic. Before long, my neighbors were no longer receiving me, and I had only my dear Samuel for companionship.

"What can we do, Samuel?" I ranted one night. "How can we keep her from killing again?"

He shook his head gloomily. "I dunno, suh. If Mary an' 'Becca cain't spell her, then I don' guess nobody can. An' I'm afraid she'll come after you next."

"Her charms have lost their magic for me, Samuel. I hope never to lay eyes on Elizabeth Rouett again."

The next morning, I found Samuel outside my door. His body still held faint traces of warmth, but his wide, staring eyes and ashen color marked the end of the only surviving person to have shared my childhood.

I moved woodenly, numbly that morning, ordering Simon to pack my trunks, giving detailed instructions to the overseer. Looking back, I see how cowardly my behavior was. But at the time, I felt I had no choice. It was either escape or be consumed by this creature whom, I now believe, was something far more fiendish than human. I went to Europe.

I stayed there for twenty long years, moving from place to place as the fancy struck me. I did not intend to stay so long; the War intervened, and travel became impossible. And, yes, I was afraid to return to my father's home. I was afraid of who—or what—waited for me at Seven Oaks. But at last I returned.

I hired a carriage to bring me and my trunks up from Mobile. I half knew what to expect at my own place. I had hired a cousin to look after the place when the overseer was drafted and then killed in the War. He had written that the fields all lay fallow and the house needed paint.

But what I did not expect was the sight of Seven Oaks, some shutters closed like blind eyes and others hanging by a hinge, a madman winking in the sun. The gravel drive was choked with weeds, and the veranda tilted drunkenly to the south.

I suppose I had imagined that Seven Oaks would be unchanged. That Elizabeth, laughing, vibrant Elizabeth, would be waiting to greet me, her small white teeth gleaming. I learned later that she had moved to Mississippi, to some property one of her husbands had owned.

But some nights when I cannot sleep and the moon draws my eye to the window, I imagine I see her still, dancing across the smooth, green lawn, whirling and laughing with joy. If I look hard enough, I can just make out the faint shadows of six masculine forms, trying without success to keep up. And behind me, at my shoulder, is the solid, loving presence of the slave who tried in vain to save me from this madness.

LOST SOUL

he thin door of the trailer shuddered like a live thing in his hand as he flung it open and flew down the stairs. He fled from the sight of his mother on her knees and the sound of her sobs. He fled into the ring of trees that enclosed the trailer, cut it off from every other living thing, from the world of normal activities, normal conversations. Once enveloped by the blackness and silence of the forest, he threw back his head and howled, a sound so filled with pain, laced through with anguish, it seemed the very moon would weep in sympathy.

It had all started over a stupid little Bic lighter. His mother, going through his dresser (again) had found it. Other mothers, he thought bitterly, might come unglued at finding a condom. A joint. A dirty magazine. Or even cigarettes. But this was just a lighter—he might have bought it for something as innocent as lighting campfires. Or candles.

Finding it, she had immediately launched a harangue that lasted until well past sunset. She began slow, just cataloging all the wicked, sinful things he might be doing with such a toy of Satan. (A lighter? Some part of his brain had shrieked incredulously. It was as common as a toothpick and about as harmful. What planet did this woman *come* from?). Then, after a good hour, she worked herself up to all the things that could lead from a lighter—smoking dope, meeting up with drug pushers, jail, turning into a junkie, on and on. (That same part of his brain, mercifully distanced from this scene, admired the elasticity of her imagination. She could reach incredible heights just by raising her eyes).

After she exhausted this list of evils, she began talking about carnal sin. (Hoo, boy, that little voice whispered, here we go.) These were the sins that came from pastimes that seemed innocent. This was how the Devil got into the souls of little boys like hers, like her little Michael, and once he got in, there was no rooting him out, no sir, only God could help (and does God listen to a madwoman? he wondered, but the thought scared him so he shut off that voice as his mother pushed down on his shoulders).

"Pray, Michael," she spit, pushing his tall (nearly six-foot) angular frame down, and he submitted because this was how his life had been as long as he could remember. She hissed some more, telling him how to pray, and then she fell to her knees too, sobbing and imploring God to spare her boy, he was innocent, it was she that sinned, and when she started like that Michael knew it was time to shut off his ears too. He repeated, over and over, mechanically, "Forgive me, God, for all my evil thoughts," but his voice was drowned out by hers.

Suddenly it seemed the cacophony of prayers and tears would drive him insane, and he bolted out the door into the night, which cloaked him even if it had no power to forgive him.

He had no tears in him. But his howls released a fraction of his pain, enough so he could fold his awkward limbs—these arms and legs that had, seemingly overnight, grown to a man's proportions—into a crouch at the foot of a massive old oak tree. There, around to the north side, was an abandoned burrow, just big enough to hold a three-ring binder carefully wrapped in a plastic Piggly Wiggly bag to keep moisture out. This was his secret life. This was the part of him his mother would never know. If she read his thoughts, it would send her imagination spiraling down to the gates of hell, pulling him along behind.

He felt this night and every night for the past six months a nameless hunger that left him breathless with its strength. It wasn't sex. He didn't need the warmth of a body next to his in that way. He'd lost his virginity a year before in a strange encounter in the woods with a girl visiting her uncle in the trailer park up the road. She'd slyly come up to him, circled his waist with her arm, and commented on his height. Then she'd spread his fingers out and screeched with delighted (or was it demented?) laughter. Then she'd asked him, bluntly, if he wanted to "do it."

Of course he did. So they did. But it wasn't much different than the relief he'd found at his own hands. Sex wasn't the cause of the strange hunger that gripped him now.

He'd tried smoking a little pot to see if the hunger would disappear, but that just made it worse. And then one day after he'd gotten high and was twisting scraps of rusted, abandoned sheet metal into fantastic shapes deep in the woods below the trailer, he'd cut his hand. Instinctively he put the cut with its glistening, swelling bead of scarlet to his mouth, and he was transformed.

Just remembering that day made him shudder and throw back his head again and cry, "What's happening to me?" He felt hot and cold and out of control, yet immensely powerful, with no outlet for his power and only the senseless, distant moon for company.

"I can help."

The voice was small. He jerked his head around and fell comically on his rear end, deciding in the same instant that he must have imagined it.

"Let me help."

"Where are you?" He was panicked. He lived a full mile away from the trailer park and six miles away from town. No one came out to these woods except himself. Especially not after dark.

"I've been watching you."

For one wild moment, he thought it was the Devil come to claim his soul, just like his mother had always said. Then she appeared from behind another oak tree, a slender waif with an unruly cloud of brownish-red hair like an aura around her delicately-featured face. She was dressed in all black: a black full skirt that whispered promises as she walked and a low-cut blouse with a flaring, full gypsy collar. Silver skulls, lizards, and other creatures swayed from a chain around her neck, making an absurdly gay sound in the dark forest.

He knew who she was. Lily. She was a senior this year and not a part of any crowd, but accepted by all. Cheerleaders, 'heads, jocks, nerds.

They were, if not respectful, at least nonjudgmental. She was known as an oddball but harmless. To him, she was beautiful.

"I've seen your sculptures. I've even read your poems. You're very talented," she said, in a tea-party kind of voice that was absurdly inappropriate for these woods, this night. She led him, unprotesting, to a patch of grass in a clearing between the trees, and they sat down. He clutched his journal tightly to his chest.

She reached for his other hand and held both of them fast. His journal dropped to the grass with the softest of noises. She leaned close to him, and he could smell her breath, with the tang of tobacco and something else.

"Michael, we're just alike. You can do what I do and be happy," she whispered. "Be with me."

Somehow, instinctively, he knew she wasn't talking about sex. This was something that meant more. Something that would, indeed, let him catch a glimpse of God's face. Or maybe something that would push him down, make him fall, make him fulfill all his mother's predictions. At that moment, holding her hands and feeling her pulse racing, he didn't care. Saved or damned, he didn't care.

Clouds had come up from nowhere and covered the face of the moon so he heard rather than saw her pull the heavy necklace over her head. When the light reappeared, he saw at one end of the chain a silver dagger, no longer than the first joint of his little finger. At the other end of the chain was a heavily carved tiny cup, a little bigger than a thimble. She handed both pieces to him, the remaining charms clattering harmlessly between them. She smiled.

"What do you want me to do, Lily?" he forced the words out of his throat. But he knew.

"I want to taste you, Michael." Reflected moonlight made her eyes glitter, and her teeth shone like little pearls as her lips parted in a smile.

His hands trembled. With his left hand he guided the dagger to the fleshy part of his right forearm. The fingers of his right hand held the tiny cup ready.

Clouds skittered across the night sky with a slightly anxious air, like mice in a room that is unexpectedly inhabited.

"Not the vein, Michael." Her hand guided the dagger away from the big blue vein that throbbed at the crook of his arm.

He cut, and it did not hurt. Crimson welled up, dropped into the little cup, and she got up on her knees to reach the wound with her lips. As she suckled gently, he became dizzy, and the stars above the treetops buzzed and swarmed like confused white bees. After what seemed like eternity, she rocked back on her knees, licked out the little cup, and smiled at him. The cut, barely a half-inch long, was no longer bleeding.

His long body was curved protectively over her as they sat, close but not quite touching, and he wished he could feel like this forever. What he had done for her, he could never do for any other. There would never be another night like this, never be another hunger like hers, never be another tongue to touch his skin the same way.

When she raised her blouse, exposing her pale breasts with the necklace hanging heavy between them, he caught his breath. "Be like me," she'd said.

Time stood still as she took the little dagger to the soft curve where her right breast just began to slope up toward the nipple. She pressed, and the supple skin resisted the blade at first, then relented. He stared, mesmerized, at the thin line of blood that slowly grew wider, until she wrapped her hand around his neck and pulled him down to drink.

Afterwards, he felt full, satiated. Her blood coursing through his body mingled with his blood, causing an effervescence that made him feel higher than anything he'd ever smoked. Made him feel more whole, more real, more anchored to the world and yet, somehow, above it, conqueror, creator, controller. The intensity of the high exhilarated him. And frightened him.

Too soon, she pulled away. Rearranged her clothes. Made him promise not to act any different toward her at school, although, with her blood inside him and his inside her, he already felt a pulling, a force that would negate his pledge no matter how he resisted.

"People don't understand us, Michael," she warned. "Don't tell!" The words hung invisible, a web before the morning dew reveals its sticky lure to the creature's hapless prey. And she was gone, leaving Michael in a world that had changed in such a fundamental way that it, incredibly, appeared exactly the same.

In the next few days, he began spending more and more time in the woods, writing poems about her and for her and to her. He wrote about the hunger she had satisfied and only slowly came to realize that she had awakened a more visceral hunger in him.

Tasting Lily had somehow given him the power to fend off his mother's own strange hungers for prayer and humiliation. He barely heard her protests as he left the trailer after meals and brushed off her pleas for shared prayers when he returned, sometimes only hours before he needed to leave for school. If she had dared, she would have kept him away from school, but the sheriff had served her with a warrant the last time she forced him to turn truant.

So he went to school and revolved, a mute planet, around the brilliant light that was Lily. Classes were mere trifles of time between seeing her, and lunch period became holy because he could wrap her up with his eyes and conjure up the sensation of her skin against his as he watched her move, converse, laugh, and eat. He never went close enough to touch her, although every nerve in his body screamed for a taste, a flicker of the tongue, or even a look that held the promise of another night like the first.

At last, one night as he huddled with his back to the oak tree, she came again. He was nearly consumed by the same hunger that heralded her first approach, but now that hunger had deepened and spread so that sometimes he would look at the pencil in his hand and wonder how it got there, or stare at the ground with the disoriented feeling that it was the sky and he was floating like a balloon that had lost its string.

It had become, he would swear, a physiological dilemma so that his pulse was slower, each breath was harder to take, as if oxygen was slowly turning into a foreign substance.

"Michael."

He set his journal down and turned toward the sound of her voice. She materialized out of the shadows as she had the first time. He reached for her, but she eluded his hands.

"Let's go."

He didn't ask where. Didn't care. As long as she was at the end of the road or just in front of him as they moved, that was all that mattered. They followed a trail through the woods, guided by the moonlight. The small penlight he used to write by was forgotten in his pocket. Eventually they arrived at the road, where a battered old Toyota Corolla waited. He slipped into the passenger seat as she started the engine and headed, not west toward town, but south toward the city of Birmingham.

It was only a forty minute ride. Each time he started to speak, she lifted her hand and placed her fingers softly against his lips. The last time she did that, he caught one between his teeth, fleetingly, before she pulled away, laughing. Once in Birmingham, she circled around the Fountain, searching for a parking place. At last, she found one, and sprang out of the car.

"Ready to go hunting, Michael?" she asked softly.

He stiffened. "Lily, I don't want to hurt anybody."

Her laugh chimed in unison with the charms dangling around her neck. "It doesn't hurt, Michael, remember?"

He hung back until, impatient, she tugged at his hand to pull him along. They approached the Fountain with its fantastic creatures, some cold iron, others flesh and blood. The human variety had spiked hair in every hue, black leather, chains, and other outward signs of an inward toughness, an inner invulnerability. Or were these trappings merely a shield for their souls' weakness? Michael wasn't sure, but he was certain of the attention Lily attracted. She exuded a sultry promise, a craving that defied clarification but intrigued women and men alike.

Following in her wake, Michael couldn't hear the whispered words with two leather-clad men in their early twenties, but he could see the flash of triumph in her eyes as she led all three men away from the busy, brightly lit Fountain to a dim alleyway beyond.

The four lounged against the walls, passing a couple of joints from one cupped hand to the next. Talk turned from this to that, until finally Lily's voice lighted, like a butterfly, on the topic that made Michael's heart beat faster.

"I met a vampire, once," she said dreamily. All three men watched, immobilized, as her hand lightly traced a path from her bright red lips down her neck.

"Did he, like, suck your blood?" said the taller stranger, leaning toward Lily as if drawn in by her presence.

"He wanted to," she said. The man was too high to hear the evasion in her careful choice of words. "Have you ever wanted to?"

"I'd like to live forever," the other guy offered. Lily didn't spare him a glance. She pinned down the first man with her eyes.

"It would be almost like a kiss," she said, her lips twisted in the barest of smiles.

He stared back, sensing a challenge but not yet knowing what dimensions it might assume.

"Almost, like, suckling a baby." Her voice had dropped so low that Michael had to strain to hear it. The busy streets around the fountain suddenly seemed light-years away; the universe had narrowed down to this one single point, a dirty narrow alley with trash cartwheeling in an infrequent breeze.

The second guy sensed something that was beyond the parameters of a world he could accept and muttered some excuse about somebody waiting to meet him. The other three barely noticed his departure.

"What's your name again?" purred Lily.

"Daniel," he said.

"Daniel," she moved close enough to touch him, and her hand snaked around his neck to pull him closer to her face. "I'd like to taste you." Her tongue flickered in and out of his ear, making him startle like a deer or a very young infant.

Michael watched, fascinated, but a little sickened, too. This was his goddess, his sun, and her power was frightening to witness. Somehow it was easier when that concentration was focused on him. When he was the one being consumed by her passion. Seeing another victim fall made his own status as prey that much closer to his consciousness.

He watched her go through the ritual with Daniel, although Daniel did not drink from her. Michael's own craving for blood was as high as it had ever been, but when she offered him the slowly oozing cut, he turned away. This was her hunt, her quarry, not his. He didn't even know if he had the heart to hunt as she did. He only knew he had the hunger.

When she was through, and they had left Daniel, dazed but not mortally wounded, in the alleyway, Lily turned to him.

"You need it, just like I do," she said as she delicately ran a fingertip around her lips to clean any stray signs of her feast.

Michael mumbled, knowing she was right but almost hating her all the same. "I need you," he said, abruptly turning and grasping her arm. "Let me, please!"

"Don't be ridiculous, Michael," she said coolly, shaking off his arm as if he had no more strength than a child. "Let's go get a drink. Maybe you'll meet a girl who's just your type."

She cut her eyes up at him and giggled, suddenly transformed into someone like the smirking, superior cheerleaders he'd carefully avoided since early adolescence. Those girls hurt. This one, he realized, has the power to hurt me like none other. The thought made him nearly retch with an agony so clear, so profound, it turned his bowels to water.

Somehow, Michael stumbled through the night, saying little and following her and her designated prey out to the alleyway two separate times. Both times, she offered him the wound to drink, but he refused in spite of the growing hunger. Finally, the bars closed for the night, and they headed back home. She ignored Michael's single, anguished plea for her blood and stopped at the edge of the woods a mile from his mother's trailer.

Michael shambled out of the car and between the trees, torn between the need to sob and the aching, empty feeling that gnawed at his midsection. He kept moving, too sick to make any sounds at all, when the glowing eyes of a feral cat stopped him in his tracks. A wild hope seized him. "Here, kitty, kitty," he said carefully. "C'mere, kitty. Pretty kitty, kitty." She approached him slowly, unsure of human intentions. As soon as his broad hands wrapped around the soft fur, he quickly snapped the animal's neck, his own tormented howl rising above her death-cry.

Sickened, but starved, he ripped the skin from the flesh and held the dripping corpse to his lips, desperately trying to slake his thirst. It only took a taste before he realized the innocent animal's death was useless. Cramps seized his stomach, and he barely had time to throw the mangled animal's body away before crumpling to his knees, vomiting blood, saliva, and beer.

After what seemed like hours of punishing pain, he managed to return to his mother's trailer and creep up the rickety stairs. She was awake and on her knees in the narrow living room. She made no comment on the time or his disheveled state, but only redoubled her cries to Jesus to save her poor sinful son.

Michael didn't make it to school the next day. Or the next. It was only on the third day that his mother literally pulled his lanky frame out of the bed, insisting that he go. Listless, pale, and suffering, he attended classes but paid no attention to the students or the teachers.

Lily ignored him. If he thought he'd been cut off from life before, now he felt surely cursed. There was not a single shred of hope left, yet he spent his evenings in the woods, waiting.

The third night, Lily returned. She slipped silently between the trees and appeared before him like a wisp of smoke. She was a wisp of hope.

"I'm leaving," she said simply.

"Why?" He felt the hope slide away, leaving an empty grayness that cried out for the color of her blood.

"There's nothing for me here. I don't want to end up like my mother. I don't want to live in a trailer in the woods," she said cruelly.

"Don't," he whispered. But she was already gone.

The moon was full again, hanging low and ripe, framed by the branches of the trees. Michael clenched his eyes so tightly shut that he saw red, the blessed red of her blood, and a moan slipped from his throat.

"Lost!" he shrieked, and the edges of his voice came unraveled. His teeth snapped down on his soft, unsuspecting inner cheek. He gnawed, and drank, but wasn't satisfied. He was irretrievably, irredeemably lost, a dark whisper of pain aloft in an unfeeling wind.